Okuden: Reiki Second Degree Manua

By Taggart King

Published by Pinchbeck Press

www.pinchbeckpress.com
Email: taggart@reiki-evolution.co.uk

ISBN 978-0-9563168-1-3

Introduction

Hi,

My name is Taggart King and I would like to welcome you to Reiki Second Degree.

You may be reading this before attending one of our live courses and in that case I would like to congratulate you for deciding to take some further steps that are going to lead to many positive changes in your life. I hope you enjoy reading about the ways that you can develop further your self-healing and treatment of others. I have tried to make this manual a complete guide to Second Degree, so there is no need to take notes on the day of your course: everything that we will cover, and everything that you need to know at this level, is in this manual and on the Audio CD which accompanies it. The manual will also act as a useful permanent reference for you once you have completed the course.

Congratulations, too, if you are reading this manual as part of your Reiki Second Degree home study course. This manual, together with the audio CD, the detailed course instructions and the e-mail support that you will receive, are all you need to get to grips with Reiki at Second Degree (Okuden) level. Your home study course is equivalent to the live course in every way and by the end of your course you will have carried out a great deal of practical energy work.

You may be reading this manual as someone who has already trained in Reiki in another lineage. In that case I hope that you find many things of use to you in this manual, which is based largely on the system that Mikao Usui was teaching in the early part of the 20th century. What Reiki's founder was teaching is very different from the Reiki system that is taught in most Western lineages, and there may be some surprises in store for you. I ask you to keep an open mind.

Finally, you may be reading this manual in order to find out about Reiki for the first time. In that case I hope you find clear and easy to understand explanations, and end up with a fair idea of what Reiki is all about at this level, and what it can do for you and the people who are close to you. I hope you decide to make Reiki part of your life.

About This Manual

I have written the vast majority of this manual. Where information has come from other sources, I have stated this clearly. I am grateful to Susie Jennings and Sue Jones, both Reiki Masters who have trained with me, who have provided useful information about Reiki and the Law and Health and Safety.

Reiki is a tradition that is passed on from master to student; the student becomes a master and passes it on to others and so on. Below you can find your Reiki lineage as far back as Mikao Usui, the originator of Reiki, and this lineage applies to people who have trained with me or with one of my team of teachers.

Acknowledgements

I would like to thank Diane Whittle, a lovely lady, for taking the time, trouble and care to introduce me to Reiki at all levels. Diane taught myself and my fellow students with gentle humour, wisdom and compassion and provided me with a solid foundation to build on. My Reiki Master attunements in the woods and on the beach in Suffolk were something very special!

During my travels throughout the UK and Europe, teaching the methods of Mikao Usui's original system, I had the honour to meet and share knowledge and experiences with many talented and experienced Reiki teachers. It would be difficult to list them all, but in particular I am grateful to Carly Horbowiec from Holland and Chris Deefholts from Oxfordshire for giving me the benefit of their wisdom and experience. I am also indebted to Frank Arjava Petter, Chetna Koyabashi, and Fiona McCallion for introducing me to Japanese-style Reiki.

In particular I need to single out Chris Marsh for thanks: the person who finally led me to real Usui Reiki by providing me with patient training over several years and offering me insights into Mikao Usui's original system, sharing things that I could not have obtained anywhere else in the world.

I would like to thank the hundreds of students who have been through my Reiki courses, who have taught me so much, and I would like to thank Margaret Craig for her help in reading through the text of this new manual and providing me with invaluable feedback.

With best wishes,

Taggart King
Reiki Master/Teacher

ReikiEvolution
5 Rose Lane, Pinchbeck, Spalding, Lincs PE11 3RN
Tel/Fax: 0845 458 3004 (Local Rates Apply) and +44 (0)1775 722082
E-Mail: taggart@reiki-evolution.co.uk
Web Sites: www.reiki-evolution.co.uk

Using the Course Audio CDs

This course is accompanied by an Audio CD which focuses you on the main points of the course, and the 'Reiki Meditations' audio CD that accompanied your First Degree course contains guided meditations that you can use to help with your symbol meditations and distant healing. The commentary should be listened to in conjunction with the corresponding sections of the course manual, rather than just being listened to in their entirety. You will learn more effectively if you use audio and visual learning together, focusing on one section of the manual at a time.

The course instructions for your home study course, or the instructions you received with your live course study pack, let you know which tracks to listen to in conjunction with which sections of the course manual.

Students' Experiences

In various parts of the manual, you can read the experiences of some of our students who have been working with the Reiki First Degree course through home study, and who have been giving detailed written feedback by e-mail. We hope that doing this will enhance your experience of the course, whether working at a distance or on a 'live' course.

It is useful to be able to see how other people have been doing with a particular exercise, what they have noticed, what they have discovered, what they were surprised about. By including such feedback in the manual you can benefit from the experiences of many people who have been working through the same exercises that you will be following.

Whenever a new student gives their feedback, the section will begin with this icon:

Lineage

All Reiki practitioners can trace their 'spiritual lineage', following a trail of Reiki teachers back to the originator of Reiki, Mikao Usui. Apparently the Reiki etiquette is to quote the lineage of the first person that attuned you to Master level as your Reiki lineage, so if someone asks you what your lineage is, then you should quote the list shown below:

If you followed a home study course with Taggart, here is your lineage:	If you attended a Reiki Evolution Live Course, here is your lineage:
Mikao Usui Chujiro Hayashi Hawayo Takata Phyllis LeiFurumoto Florence O'Neal Jerry Farley June Woods Simon Treselyan Marcus Hayward Diane Whittle Taggart King … your name goes here …	Mikao Usui Chujiro Hayashi Hawayo Takata Phyllis LeiFurumoto Florence O'Neal Jerry Farley June Woods Simon Treselyan Marcus Hayward Diane Whittle Taggart King … your teacher's name goes here … … your name goes here …

I have various other Reiki lineages, where I have received attunements and informal training from several Reiki teachers in Europe, all variations on Mrs Takata's "Western" style of Reiki. I have also trained in more Japanese-style Reiki with Frank Arjava Petter and I have been taught various techniques that Reiki Master Hiroshi Doi has presented in the West.

One lineage of special note involves my having received empowerments and instruction from Chris Marsh; these empowerments pass on the energy of Usui Sensei through the intermediary of a Tendai Buddhist nun – Suzuki San - who trained with Usui and is now over 100 years old; I received ongoing training from Chris for several years. This would be the most direct transmission:

Mikao Usui
Suzuki San
Chris Marsh
Taggart King

Following the System

What did Mikao Usui teach?

Since the 1990s Reiki has been going through some changes in many quarters. Until then everyone had assumed that the Reiki that Mikao Usui taught was the same as the Reiki that Mrs Takata had been teaching: in fact her teachings are usually referred to as "traditional" Usui Reiki. It was thought that Reiki had died out in Japan, and that the only Reiki that had survived was the system that Mrs Takata had been teaching. But the 1990s ushered in a new stage in Reiki's development, when information started to filter through from Japan, in dribs and drabs, from different sources. Some information made sense, some seemed confusing, a lot of the information contradicted what people had believed about Reiki, and some of the information was inconsistent or contradictory.

Over time, though, we have built up more of a consistent picture of what Usui Sensei's system was all about, what he taught and how he taught it, though you can find books that contain the earlier – now contradicted – view of what Usui's system was all about. The main confusion arose when the Usui Reiki Ryoho Gakkai (Usui Memorial Society) was discovered. Everyone thought that this society had been founded by Usui himself and that it had continued Usui Sensei's system in its original form, but now we know that the society was set up after his death by the Imperial Officers, who had been taught a system that was not representative of the system that Usui had been teaching to the majority of his students, and we know that the Imperial Officers changed and altered what they had been taught early on in the 'Gakkai's history. 'Gakkai Reiki proved to be very different from Usui Reiki.

We discovered that Usui's system was not called "Reiki". In fact the system had no real name. Usui seems to have referred to his system as a 'Method to Achieve Personal Perfection', and some of his students seem to have called the system 'Usui Teate' (teate means 'hand application' or 'hand healing') or 'Usui Do' (way of Usui). The word Reiki appeared in the Reiki precepts, but the word 'Reiki' seems there to mean 'a system that has been arrived at through a moment of enlightenment', or 'a gift of satori'. The name 'Reiki' as a description of system came later, and may have been used first when the naval officers set up the Usui Reiki Ryoho Gakkai.

We also discovered that the purpose of Usui's method was to achieve satori, to find one's spiritual path, to heal oneself. Usui's system was not really about treating others. Treating others was not emphasised; it was not focused upon; it was a side issue. This came as rather a shock to a Reiki world that saw Reiki as a hands-on treatment method first and foremost.

The Original System

The information that we have about the system that Mikao Usui taught has come mainly from a group of surviving students who are in contact with one or two people in the West. They were twelve in number when they were first discovered, though I understand that now – in 2005 – there are only a handful of them left. These are people who knew Usui, trained with him, and passed on his teachings to others in a quiet and limited fashion. Their information has helped to 'make sense' of the sometimes confusing and contradictory information from other sources in Japan, and they paint a picture of a simple spiritual system that is very different from the treatment-based Reiki that we see routinely in the West.

So the original Japanese form of Reiki is very different from the way that it has ended up being practised in the West. The thing that strikes me most about original Usui Reiki is the fact that it is so simple, so elegant, powerful and uncluttered. The system is not bogged down in endless mechanical techniques and complex rituals that now clutter up a lot of Western-style Reiki, with endless rules and regulations and restrictions.

The prime focus of Mikao Usui's Reiki was the personal benefits that would come through committing oneself to working with the system, in terms of self-healing and spiritual development. Reiki was a path to enlightenment. Healing others was a minor aspect of the system, not emphasised, not focused upon; it was simply something that you could do if you followed Usui's system.

Original Usui Reiki involved committing yourself to carrying out daily energy exercises, self-healings, and receiving spiritual empowerments on a regular basis. You would have received training in an open ended fashion, rather like the way that martial arts is taught in the West today: you kept turning up and slowly developing your skills, and when it was thought that you had progressed sufficiently, you were allowed to move on to the next level.

The system was rooted in Tendai Buddhism and Shintoism, with Tendai Buddhism providing spiritual teachings and Shintoism contributing methods of controlling and working with the energies. The system was based on living and practising the Reiki precepts. The vast majority of Usui's students started out as his clients – he was well known as a healer, though what he taught was not really a treatment method. He would routinely give people empowerments so that they could treat themselves in between appointments, and if they wanted to take things further then they could start formal training with him, to learn how to heal themselves.

Before I detail what Usui Sensei taught at Second Degree level, and how we can echo this system, I want to take a slight detour by describing how Second Degree is taught in 'standard' Western-style 'Takata' Reiki, as distorted and mutated as it has passed from teacher to teacher over the years.

'Standard' Western-style Second Degree

Western-style Reiki is very much presented as a hands-on treatment technique, with an undercurrent of spirituality and self-healing, and Second Degree is no exception. Western Second Degree involves being 'attuned' to three symbols and there is a widespread belief that the symbols are useless – they will not work for you – until you have been 'attuned' to them on the day of the live course.

Students are taught how to use these symbols when giving Reiki treatments and when carrying out distant healing, though there is no real consensus about how the symbols should be used – this differs in different lineages. There tend to be quite a few rules and dogma concerning how the symbols must, and must not, be used, and symbol use tends to be quite complicated, with mixtures of symbols and symbol 'sandwiches' being taught routinely (see later).

The symbols tend not to be used when self-treating.

Students are usually not shown how to experience the energy of a particular symbol, because they are taught to mix the symbols together all the time, often in an arbitrary and illogical fashion.

This contrasts greatly with Mikao Usui's system, as passed on to us by his surviving students. What I am going to do below is to just recap briefly what Usui Sensei's First Degree training was all about, and then I will move on to describe what was passed on at Second Degree level, and how we can echo that original approach.

Mikao Usui's First Degree (Shoden)

Mikao Usui's First Degree training ("Shoden", which means 'first teachings') was very simple, and it seems that Usui taught hundreds of people at this level. Shoden was all about opening to the energy through receiving many Reiju empowerments (simple connection rituals), it was about cleansing and self-healing.

The student would practice different forms of self-healing, including self-healing meditations, they would chant and live the Reiki affirmations, and they would practice a couple of energy exercises.

Students would be introduced to the concept of mindfulness, they would focus on developing their awareness of their Tanden and that would, for some, lead to second-degree level.

Students would not treat others at first-degree.

Mikao Usui's Second Degree (Okuden)

We know that the precepts provided the foundation of Usui Sensei's system, so students would continue to live their lives in accordance with these principles, as well as continuing to practise mindfulness, which was emphasised more at this level. They would continue to receive regular empowerments from Usui, and indeed regular empowerments continued throughout the students' training at all levels.

So far, then, Second Degree has continued with the basic approach established at First Degree, and what was different at Okuden level was the spiritual teachings the students received, and the energy work that they carried on for an extended period of time. The energy work was carried out for the purpose of furthering the students' self-healing and spiritual development, though the energies that were worked with could also have been used to treat people.

Some treatments might have been carried out by some of Usui's students but this wasn't really emphasised, and any treatments would have been carried out simply, using intuition, and without the application of 'techniques'.

Usui's Second Degree was split into two sub-levels - Okuden Zenki and Okuden Kouki - with perhaps 70 students having reached Zenki and maybe 30 of those having reached Kouki level.

The energy work at Second Degree furthered your self-healing and spiritual development by allowing you to fully experience your physical reality and your spiritual essence, and allowing you to experience a state of oneness, a powerful process for helping to achieve balance. The energy work was carried out by the students using meditations, or chanting sacred sounds, though a few of the students used symbols.

The Spiritual teachings introduced at Second Degree level involved studying Buddhist sutras: the Lotus sutra, the Heart sutra and the Diamond sutra. The Lotus sutra is the foundation document of Tendai Buddhism, and it seems that Usui Sensei was passing on the inner teachings of Tendai Buddhism in a way that could be understood by everyone. Usui did not expect his students to have a particular religious background, though, and we do not have details of the spiritual teachings that Usui was passing on.

Zenki

In the first of the two second-degree levels (Zenki) you would practise 'becoming' the energies of earth ki and heavenly ki, two fundamental energies that are used and referred to in Taoism, Buddhism, Shinto, and in energy practices like QiGong and Tai Chi. You would do this by practising various meditations over many months, or by chanting sacred sounds and meditating on the energies that they elicited, or maybe a bit of both approaches. You learned to 'become' these energies over an extended period of time in order to move along your path to enlightenment, and to promote self-healing. This process was not rushed, since you had to learn to 'become' the energies fully, one energy at a time. Students would have worked with each energy for perhaps 6-9 months before moving on, so it was a slow process; the two energies that were introduced at Okuden Zenki had to be fully integrated before you moved on to Okuden Kouki.

The sacred sounds that you used to further your self-healing and spiritual development could also be used to treat others, and students might do some treatments at this level, though it was a bit of a sideline to the main thrust of the system. Treatments might be based on a few simple hand positions that were used on the head, though this was not taught to all students, and the focus was very much on intuition in terms of hand-placement and in terms of what energy – if any – you emphasised during the treatment.

The sacred sounds, called 'Kotodama' (or 'Jumon' if referred to from a Buddhist perspective), come from Shintoism, the indigenous religion of Japan. This is really ancient stuff. This takes us back to the mists of ancient Japanese history, to a time when the sound of the human voice was said to be able to stop armies, to kill, to heal and to control the weather.

The use of the Reiki Kotodama is covered on the Reiki Evolution "Deepening" course and the Reiki Master / Teacher course.

Kouki

At this second sublevel of Second Degree you would be introduced to the concept of oneness, which was one of the goals of the system, and you would learn through carrying out meditations, and/or chanting one of the Reiki Kotodama, to fully experience 'oneness'. Distance healing as practised in the West is an expression of oneness, and Usui's students would have realised that they could do this easily, though again this was a sideline to the main thrust of the system and in fact I do not think there is any evidence of the original students having carried out distant healing as we would understand it. I think that their view would have been that if all are one, if there is no me and there is no you, then working on your self is the same as working on other people.

Actually, treating other people is an expression of oneness too!

The Use of Symbols in Usui's system

Interestingly, no symbols entered into Usui's system for the majority of his students. The Reiki symbols were introduced into the system late in Usui Sensei's life, they were introduced jointly by Usui and his senior student and friend Toshihiro Eguchi, and they were introduced for the benefit of the Imperial Officers, including Dr Chujiro Hayashi. Usui was well known as a healer, though his system was not about treating others, and he had been approached by the Japanese military who wanted Usui to teach a simple hands-on healing system that could be used by Imperial Naval officers in a navy that had woefully inadequate levels of medically-trained staff.

So Usui passed on to them a system that was focused on the treatment of others and which, instead of requiring students to meditate or chant for many, many months in order to get to grips with certain energies, utilised symbols as a quick way of representing those energies in a treatment context. The Imperial Officers simply did not have the time to get to grips with the energies in the way that the other students had, and it seems that they were not so interested in the self-healing and spiritual development aspects of the system that Usui had taught to all the other students.

Since Dr Hayashi passed his modified version of these teachings onto Mrs Takata, and Mrs Takata passed on her interpretation of these teachings in the West, we have ended up with a Reiki with a heavy 'treatment-of-others' slant, and a system based on the use of symbols when treating people at Second Degree level. The meditations and the sacred sounds that Usui taught to most of his students simply did not make the journey to the West with Mrs Takata.

But since the symbols are there to represent the energies of earth ki and heavenly ki, we can use the symbols when meditating to experience these energies, in the same way that the earlier students used sacred sounds, for example, to fully 'become' the energies of earth ki and heavenly ki. You can find out how to meditate on the symbols later in the manual.

How can we follow the teachings?

We know that the system that Mikao Usui taught to the majority of his students at Second Degree was a spiritual development and self-healing practice, based on these five areas:

1. Focusing on and living Mikao Usui's precepts
2. Practising mindfulness
3. Receiving Reiju empowerments regularly
4. Working with the energies of earth ki and heavenly ki
5. Experiencing a state of oneness

These areas can form the basis of our Reiki practice too. Now obviously we are not going to learn and practise Reiki in exactly the same way as was done in 1920s Japan. This is simply not possible since we live in the 21st Century in the West. We do not have the same history or cultural and spiritual background as Usui Sensei's students, and we do not know the precise details of everything that Mikao Usui taught.

But what we can do is to make part of our routine the basic practices of Usui Sensei's system, which was designed by him to be accessible to people from different backgrounds. Below I have touched on the five areas, and in subsequent chapters I will go into more details about how we can follow Usui Sensei's simple system in the modern world.

Reiju empowerments

Mikao Usui's students received empowerments from him again and again throughout their training at all levels. The training was more like martial arts style training, with ongoing and sometimes sporadic contact between student and teacher – rather than the day-courses or two-day-courses that are usual in the West (and usual in Japan now, for that matter).

But we can echo the practice of giving and receiving empowerments over an extended period as follows:

Live Reiki Courses	Reiki Home Study Courses
By receiving several Reiju empowerments from your teacher on the day of your live course	By receiving distant empowerments sent to you specifically by your teacher, during the course of your home study programme
Subsequently, by receiving distant empowerments on a weekly basis	Subsequently, by receiving distant empowerments on a weekly basis

It is simply not practical, given the distances that many people travel to attend live Reiki courses, or given the distance between many home study course students and their teacher, for the teacher and student to get together every week so that the student can receive a 'live' Reiju empowerment from the teacher.

But, since there is no difference between a 'live' Reiju empowerment and one received at a distance, we can effectively echo this original practice of empowering on a regular basis, so long as the student is prepared to commit a few minutes each week tuning into the distant empowerments which we Taggart sends out, and which can be 'tuned into' any time on a Monday.

Mikao Usui's Precepts and Mindfulness

The foundation of Usui Sensei's system was to follow a simple set of rules to live by. These 'precepts' are Buddhist or Shugendo in origin, have a very long history, and it was said that by following the precepts the student would obtain more spiritual development than was possible by carrying out any of the energy work. So the precepts – and the idea of mindfulness which is strongly linked to or suggested by the precepts – are a very important part of Mikao Usui's spiritual system and should not be glossed over.

They are the very foundation of his system. You start with the precepts.

Please go back to your First Degree manual and re-read the section that deals with the precepts and mindfulness. Read the mindfulness books that are recommended there and reaffirm your commitment to make the precepts the way that you live your life. Make mindfulness a way of life.

Working with earth ki and heavenly ki

You will already have established a regular routine of working on yourself, using Hatsurei ho and the Self-treatment meditation. Now we can modify this routine and introduce a regular practice of meditation on two Reiki symbols, to allow you to fully experience earth ki and heavenly ki, the energies of our physical reality and our spiritual essence. We do this to further our self-healing and spiritual development. These meditations, not surprisingly, focus on the Tanden, the centre of our personal universe, and you will have been focusing on your Tanden since you started your First Degree course. The symbol meditations are described later, and you will have received an audio CD containing a guided meditation that you can use to help you get to grips with this exercise.

Experiencing a state of oneness

At Second Degree we can learn to experience a state of oneness by using one of the Reiki symbols, and to cultivate this state when carrying out distant healing: a way of using oneness in practice. Oneness is a state that we can also cultivate when treating others.

Treating others at Second Degree level

In a world where Reiki is presented to the world as a sort of complementary therapy, something that you do to other people, we need to continually remind ourselves that the treatment of other people was not what Usui's system was all about. Treating others was not focused upon or emphasised. At First Degree level, Usui's students would probably have just worked on themselves. They might have treated others at Second Degree level.

But there is a world of difference between the often dogmatic, complex and 'technique-heavy' treatment approach of many Western Second Degree courses, and the simple and intuitive approach adopted by Usui Sensei and his students. We can treat more in the original way by embracing intuitive working, and you will be learning a simple method that you can use to open yourself to your intuitive side. Reiki is presented to the world as a treatment technique and this course gives you what you need to treat others confidently and successfully, moving beyond standard hand positions to go 'freestyle', gearing your treatments towards the individual energy needs of the people you are working on.

Reiki Evolution courses and their content

The logo to the left says "Shin Reiki", which translates approximately as "Reiki Evolution". So I suppose you could refer to the form of Reiki that you learn on this course as "Shin Reiki" but the last thing I want to do is to promote yet another version of Reiki with a different name! What I have done with all my Reiki courses is to blend the Western approach to Reiki teaching (day-courses rather than martial-arts style teaching, with a system based on the treatment of others) with simple and powerful methods that were part of the system developed by the founder, Mikao Usui, but which were never taught in the West.

Reiki was modified and changed a great deal during its journey to the West, through Dr Chujiro Hayashi and Mrs Hawayo Takata, and then changed again as it passed through the New Age movement and from teacher to teacher in the West. What I have tried to do is to complete the circle by bringing my teaching more in line with what seems to have been intended by Mikao Usui. I have kept the Western teaching format (day courses) but I have added a home study element to the live courses so that the student has the opportunity for the information to sink in and to carry out some simple energy work over - usually - several weeks, depending on the interval between receiving their booking and the date of their live course. Home study students follow a course that is perhaps more in line with the teaching approach that Mikao Usui used, by following a course of study and energy work over at least a six week period. I have also made sure that the courses are in sympathy with the 'treatment' emphasis of most Reiki courses.

I have adapted and changed my Reiki by, as far as I can, bringing it into line with the system that Usui set down in the early part of last century, but presenting it to you in the Western teaching format, and in a way that is compatible with other people's Reiki Second Degree courses.

The information in this manual is partly based on the traditions of Western Reiki, as taught to me by a variety of Western Masters, partly based on some of the teachings of the Usui Reiki Ryoho Gakkai in Japan (Mikao Usui's Reiki Association) which have come to us through Frank Arjava Petter and Hiroshi Doi, but mainly based on information coming from a group of Usui's surviving students, through Chris Marsh. This last source takes us the closest to Usui Sensei's original form.

Reiju

In your First Degree manual you can read all about Reiju empowerments, what they are, where they come from, how they were used by Mikao Usui and how they differ from 'attunements'. You can read about the effectiveness of distant connections and the benefits that accrue through receiving distant empowerments regularly. Perhaps you would like to start by quickly re-reading that section of the Shoden manual to refresh your memory.

Now, you know that, at First Degree, empowerments can be seen as a way of 'connecting' you to the energy, or a way of allowing you to recognise something that is within. At Second Degree, of course, you are already 'connected' to or channelling Reiki, and have been for some time, so the empowerments that you receive on this course – or the distant empowerments that you receive during your home study course – are not so much about 'connecting' you, but are more about helping to reinforce that connection. People often notice that after receiving their Second Degree empowerments the energy seems to flow more strongly, and this is frequently noticeable to the people that you have been treating.

The Second Degree empowerments 'flag up' to your energy system certain energies or states that are going to be helpful to you in terms of your self-healing and spiritual development, energies which you can continue to work with by meditating on and using the Reiki symbols, or using the Reiki Kotodama which you will learn on the Reiki Deepening course or the Master / Teacher course. The symbols act as 'triggers' that allow you to access the energies that have been strongly flagged up to your system by the empowerments you receive as part of this course.

Most people within the world of Reiki will have not received Reiju empowerments but will have received a series of 'attunements'. Many people believe that the Reiki symbols will not work for a student until they have been 'attuned' to them (by the Reiki teacher visualising that the symbols are placed into the student in some way during the attunement ritual). For most of Reiki's history, all Reiki connection rituals involved putting symbols into the student in some way, so no-one knew how to attune without using symbols, to see whether you really needed to be 'attuned' to the symbols for them to work for you.

But from Japan came Reiju, a connection ritual that does not involve the use of symbols, and we now know that you do not need to be 'attuned' to a symbol for it to work for you: you just need to be 'connected' to Reiki, and now we can achieve that without using symbols, by using Reiju. In fact once you have been attuned to Reiki then any symbol will push the energy in a particular direction without you having to have been 'attuned' to it (whatever that means).

Mikao Usui didn't attune anyone to anything.

At Second Degree you will receive three empowerments on your live course or home study course, and these empowerments tie in with the three symbols that you learn, transferring the 'essence' of the energy or state that each symbol represents. Sometimes people find that the empowerment they receive for the first symbol, for example, gives them sensations and experiences that echo the sensations and experiences they have subsequently when meditating on that symbol/energy. When they receive the empowerment that floods the student with the energy represented by the second symbol, they may have some experiences that echo the experiences they will have when they move on to meditate on that symbol/energy.

The three empowerments that you receive serve to flood you with earth ki, with heavenly ki, and to induce a state of oneness for a short while, and the empowerments are carried out in that order: earth ki, heavenly ki, oneness.

Experiencing Earth Ki and Heavenly Ki

So, we know that the original system, even at Second Degree, was still all about working on the self, self-healing and spiritual development, and we know that students at this level would spend many months experiencing earth ki and heavenly ki, spending 6-9 months meditating on earth ki and then moving on to spend a similar period of time working with heavenly ki. Most students used special meditations or chanted sacred sounds to experience these energies, but the symbols were introduced towards the end of Usui Sensei's life as a way of depicting the two energies and we can use the Reiki symbols to experience the energies of earth and heaven.

As well as being a way of experiencing these energies, the symbols can be used as 'triggers' to elicit the two energies when treating others (see later). What I am going to do in this section is to introduce you to two symbols, show you how to draw them, how to say their names, and how to use these symbols in meditations that will help you to experience earth ki and heavenly ki.

How to Draw the Reiki Symbols

Whenever you use the Reiki symbols for meditation, you will be doing these things:

- Imagining the symbol by drawing the symbol in your mind's eye, seeing the symbol being traced as if drawing it by hand with a pen or brush
- You can imagine that the symbol is being traced in violet if you like – the colour most commonly associated with the Reiki energy. If you cannot visualise colours, don't worry too much about this
- Then say the symbol's name silently to yourself, three times, as a mantra
- The combination of drawing the symbol and saying the symbol's name three times 'activates' the symbol and produces its effect

Once you have had a great deal of practice in drawing out the symbols, and they become second nature to you, you can produce the desired effect by visualising the symbol in its entirety if you can, and you can dispense with imagining each 'pen stroke'. There are no short-cuts in Reiki, though, so don't take the above advice as meaning that you don't have to bother learning how to draw out the symbols according to the correct order of their lines: when you have drawn them 500 times, then you might think about 'seeing them' in their entirety. Don't run before you can walk!

The First Symbol: Cho Ku Rei – earth ki

Pronunciation Guide

Cho,   pronounced like this: 'show'
Ku,   pronounced like this: 'koo'
Rei,   pronounced like this: 'ray'

Even emphasis on all syllables

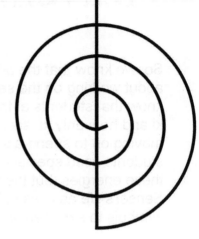

Drawing Instructions

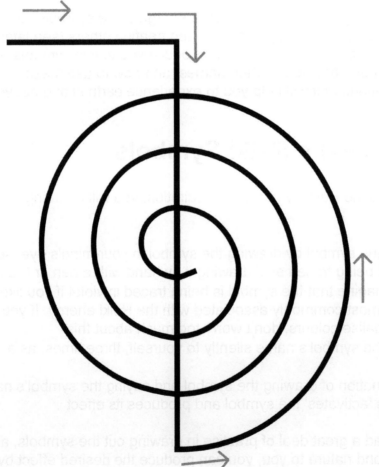

The Second Symbol: Sei He Ki - heavenly ki

Pronunciation Guide

Sei,   pronounced like this: 'say'
He,   pronounced like this: 'hay'
Ki,   pronounced like this: 'key'

Even emphasis on all syllables

Drawing Instructions

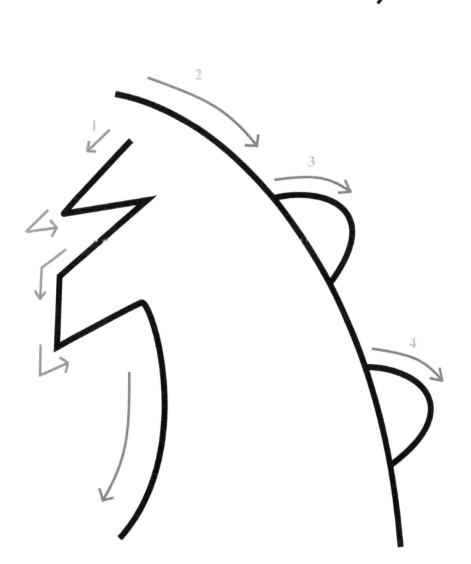

Where did the symbols come from?

This is not completely clear, but we can say that these were existing symbols introduced into the system jointly by Mikao Usui and Toshihiro Eguchi. They were not something new, invented by Usui.

ChoKuRei (usually abbreviated to CKR) means 'by divine decree' and has correspondences in Shintoism, where the phrase is used as an order (e.g. 'let there be sunshine… ChoKuRei'). It is also found in Tendai Buddhism, with an indefinite spiral.

SeiHeKi (usually abbreviated to SHK) is found all over Japan in its calligraphic form, and can be found in India and Tibet too, in Buddhist temples. The symbol we use is a line version of the Japanese symbol, which in itself is a Japanese version of a letter from the Sanskrit alphabet, the sound of which, when chanted, is said to produce 'mental spring cleaning'.

Why do I need to experience earth ki and heavenly ki?

We know that Reiki is associated with Buddhism, though we do not need to embrace Buddhism, or any religious beliefs, in order to practise Reiki. One of the goals of Buddhism is to 'experience things as they really are', so Usui Sensei gave his students the tools to use to help them to experience things as they really are, in terms of their physical reality and their spiritual essence. The view would be that what we are is physical reality and spiritual essence, and coming to fully experience these two fundamental aspects of ourselves is a powerful process for achieving balance. Thus CKR elicits an energy that relates to our physical reality, our physical existence, it is an energy that reminds us where we are from, and SHK elicits an energy that makes a link with the spiritual, drawing the two energies into harmony.

The ultimate reality is that of oneness, and Usui gave his students the tools to use to experience this state too.

Energy Meditations

So we meditate on CKR and SHK because this is a powerful self-healing method and it allows us to develop further with the Reiki system. Through meditation we become familiar with the characteristic energies of CKR and SHK, the energies of earth ki and heavenly ki. Most people in the world of Reiki will never have experienced the characteristic energies of ChoKuRei and SeiHeKi because they are not taught to use these energies by way of self-healing and because they are always taught to use the symbols together, sometimes mixed up in complicated 'sandwiches' with other symbols and in different sequences, one symbol visualised upon another when treating people. If we want our experience of Reiki to echo that of Usui's students, we need to spend time 'becoming' the energies of earth and heaven. We do this:

1. Because it is an effective self-healing practice
2. Because it allows us to develop spiritually
3. Because it reinforces our connection to the energies that we can use when treating others.

Now that you have the symbols, and have been connected strongly to the energies, it is useful for you to become familiar with the stuff that you are working with, so practice these exercises on a regular basis, instead of the self-treatment meditation. Don't stop carrying out the self-treatment meditation completely, but substitute the symbol meditation for it regularly.

How will the energies feel when I meditate on them?

You will realise that people's experiences of energy differ greatly, and what one person experiences can be very different from that experienced by other people carrying out the same exercise. There is no 'right' way to experience the energies that CKR and SHK elicit. Having said that, though, there is a general trend, a similar theme that runs through people's descriptions of the energies elicited by these two symbols.

People usually describe ChoKuRei energy as being heavy, thick, solid, and coarse, like treacle. This is because ChoKuRei elicits or brings up within us the energy of the physical body, the energy of physical reality; it is a physical healing energy. If you want to imagine that the energy resonates at different frequencies then you can imagine this energy as low frequency energy, suitable for healing the physical body. Because you feel things with your physical body, the energy of ChoKuRei is often more easily noticeable to you than the energy of SHK. The energy can feel strong and powerful, and because of this the symbol is often referred to as "The Power Symbol". This symbol is not more powerful than SHK, its energy is just different and complementary to that of SHK.

By contrast, people usually describe SeiHeKi energy as being light, delicate, fine or wispy. This is the energy of our spiritual essence, an energy that brings harmony. If you want to imagine that the energy resonates at different frequencies then you can imagine this energy as a high frequency energy that resonates at the level of our thoughts and emotions and thus is more suitable for balancing the mental and emotional aspects of a person. Because SeiHeKi 'vibrates' at a higher 'frequency' than the frequency of the physical body, the energy of this symbol is less easy to discern, less blatant, though it is no less powerful than ChoKuRei. It just feels that way usually.

Focusing on the Tanden

The energy exercises will focus on an area of your body called the "Tanden" ("Dantien" or "Tan T'ien" in Chinese) which is an energy centre located two fingerbreadths (3 – 5cm) below your tummy button and 1/3rd of the way into your body. You will be imagining that you are drawing energy – or light – into the Tanden and then moving the energy on elsewhere.

The Tanden point is seen as the centre of our selves from the Oriental point of view, a seat of power, the centre of our intuitive faculties, the centre of life. Drawing energy into your Tanden is drawing energy into the centre of your life and soul. This area acts as a power centre that allows the amazing feats of martial artists to be performed, but also acts as the source of inspiration in Oriental flower arranging and calligraphy. Meditation, exercise techniques like Tai Chi and QiGong, martial arts and Usui Reiki can all develop the Tanden.

The Tanden is thus seen as your personal energy store, the focus of your personal power. In energy cultivation techniques like Tai Chi and Qi Gong the Tanden is the place where you store the energy that you are cultivating. Conversely, martial artist might draw down energy from the sun to store in their Tanden before moving on to spar with an opponent.

The Tanden is also seen as the centre of your intuition and your creativity, so when people carry out Japanese calligraphy, or Ikebana (flower arranging) or the Tea ceremony, they are focusing their attention on the Tanden, the centre of their being.

Symbol meditation focused on the Tanden

Here is a way of experiencing the energies of the symbols through meditation, and this should be carried out for 3-5 minutes for each symbol. We recommend that you follow this meditation, focused on the Tanden, rather than the alternative method which follows…

1. Sit comfortably with your eyes closed, with your hands resting in your lap and your palms facing upwards.
2. Visualise, say, SHK up in the air above you and say the symbol's name three times silently to yourself to 'empower' the symbol.
3. As you breathe in, draw energy down from the symbol. The energy passes through your crown, down the centre of your body to your Tanden.
4. As you pause before exhaling, feel the energy getting stronger in your Tanden.
5. As you exhale, flood the energy throughout your body.

You will have noticed that this exercise is a variation on Joshin Kokkyu Ho, but we have added the focus on a Reiki symbol. The symbol, imagined up in the air above you, represents the source of the energy, and doing this is a way of saying to yourself 'I just want the energy of earth ki to flow through me'.

You visualise the symbol at the beginning of the exercise and you do not need to keep the symbol clear in your mind's eye for every second of the meditation. Visualising with a definite intent at the commencement of the exercise is sufficient, though you may choose to 'renew' the symbol by drawing it out again and saying its name to yourself three times again, at some stage during the meditation. But do not go overboard with repeating the symbol as you meditate: this is unnecessary.

How do you feel? What sensations or impressions are you getting? How does the energy affect you in terms of your physical sensations and impressions, your mental state, your mental activity, your emotions?

Meditation not focused on Tanden

Here is an alternative, which could also be carried for 3-5 minutes for each symbol:

1. Sit comfortably with your eyes closed, with your hands resting in your lap and your palms facing upwards.
2. Visualise, say, SHK up in the air above you and say the name three times silently to yourself to empower the symbol.
3. Imagine cascades of energy flooding down onto you from the symbol. The energy radiates onto your face, your torso and into your hands, flooding over you and flowing through your whole body. The energy surrounds and engulfs you.

How do you feel? What sensations or impressions are you getting? How does the energy affect you in terms of your physical sensations and impressions, your mental state, your mental activity, your emotions?

Feeling the symbols' energies in your hands

There is an exercise that you can carry out to help to experience their effects in your hands; it is called a 'palm' exercise. What you do is as follows:

Sit comfortably in a chair. You are going to be drawing a symbol with one hand and resting the other hand palm up in your lap. Bunch your fingers together into a cone and draw ChoKuRei in the air above your palm, say the name three times ("ChoKuRei, ChoKuRei, ChoKuRei") and imagine the symbol passing into your palm. After a little while you may feel something happening in your palm, or hand.

Wait for 30 seconds or so and then repeat (draw the symbol, say the name three times, and send the symbol into your palm). Does the sensation intensify or change?

After another 30 seconds or so you can repeat again if you wish.

What happened? Could you feel a change in the energy in your hands, and were there any characteristic sensations?

Now try this using SHK. How does your impression of this energy differ from that of CKR?

Students' experiences of meditating on CKR and SHK

"CKR solitary exercises: energy seemed weighty, heavy and dense. Flow down the body felt thick (like molasses). Everything seemed to slow down, and I became more restful. I often felt deep heavy pulsing in my hands. Once it felt cold, then I felt burning hot prickers on my arms as I breathed out for many breaths.

"SHK feels lighter and similar to a fast vibration (shimmery comes to mind), compared to the heavy, deep, slow throbbing feeling of CKR. Sometimes I would see very simple light patterns with CKR and complicated eye patterns with SHK."
Karen Small, USA

"During the practical exercises, the first few days it was difficult to distinguish anything between the 2 symbols. However, the sensations have become more apparent : using Chokurei the sensation of warmth is quite strong, using Sei he ki, I can feel a tingling sensation in the palm. It is very nice to feel the difference between the two symbols at this stage. I also feel very relaxed when doing the exercises.

"The meditation exercises have been really amazing for me. Again i have seen colours mainly blue but also a very strong pure white color (a bit hard to explain, it is not a proper white). I felt extremely relaxed and on one occasion i thought i was falling asleep because it felt so good. I also had a nice warm feeling. Even though there was building noise around, i could concentrate deeply on the meditation exercises and the symbols.

"...When doing my Chokurei meditation, i keep getting the impression that something is pressing on the top my head and on a few occasions, it has been quite uncomfortable. Also, I get pains and needles in on knee (left knee) and sometimes it's like being pricked with a needle.

"When doing my Sei he ki meditation, i always get a strong heat in the middle of my hands and quite often a cold breeze down my neck. I have also noticed that my breathing is different."
Bruno Cassani, Essex

"When I meditate with CKR it feel like a sudden rush of highly charged energetic entering my body, and it makes me feel more alive and relaxed at the same time. on my palms it feels very hot and buzzing as it enters into the energy. As I think about CKR my hands start to buzz and get very hot too.

"…Amazing things are happening again with the energy, I definitely feel a difference between CKR (which feels like a wave crashing against a rock) when I connect to it and SHK (which feels like gentle waves washing over me) when I'm connected to it."
Niki Leach, Tyne & Wear

"The palm exercises were magic! Notes I've made include terms like 'pins and needles in my hand' to 'feeling like my hand was bubbling'. Later in the week, I could feel a build up of energy, the energy getting stronger, each time I drew CKR over my palm. Reiki never ceases to amaze me. I found myself laughing whilst doing this, just in pleasant surprise of what was going on. Great.

"The meditation exercises were also strong, with #1 being stronger, possibly due to the assistance of the cd. Generally, my forehead was very tingly, as were my hands, fingers and wrists. Tingling also on sides and at a specific spot on the back of the head.

"Hard to describe the CKR energy any other way than 'big'. It was/is a big energy, and that's what I feel when I work with it.

"…With SHK I felt a gentler version of CKR, a sensation, but not as strong. That said, my palms were 'buzzy' and the overall sensations increased as the meditation increased. CKR was strong on the face. Also, I went into a deeper, calmer state, almost like I forgot who I was, but in a refreshing way with SHK. So yes, I discerned a notable difference between the two energies."
Jason Brown, Wales

"My experience of using the ChoKuRei energy has been interesting. I have felt a definite change in the quality of the energy when doing the palm exercise. It felt like the same pulsing energy that I feel in my head when doing the self treatments, except also accompanied with heat, and a pins and needles type sensation. When carrying out the solitary meditations it felt stronger when drawing the energy down to my dantien rather than the other method… maybe because I am now more familiar with this through the meditation.

"I have felt an increase in the amount of heat emanating from my hands and this was confirmed after treating a recipient with the ChoKuRei energy.

"There have been a few other subtle events that have taken place over the past week or so, suffice it to say that I have been feeling stronger and more energetic both physically and mentally."
Deborah Hartley, London

"I have been concentrating on meditating on the symbols and trying to experience their different energies. It took a little while, but then it seems to with me! I found CKR quite enveloping but very 'cosy' if that makes sense. SHK was much more elusive but when I did self treatments I felt very much calmer when I used it. "
Gill Oliver, Surrey

Experiencing Oneness

Some of Usui Sensei's Second Degree students moved on to the second sub-level of Second Degree, where they were introduced to the concept of oneness and given ways of experiencing this state. Oneness was seen as one of the goals of Usui's system and is an experience of ultimate reality, from a Buddhist perspective. By the time that Reiki had been taught in the West, this principle had 'morphed' into the practice of distant healing.

Usui Sensei did not actually teach distant healing and would not have thought in terms of 'connecting' to another person. He believed in the oneness of all things: we are all one so we do not need to connect to another person: we are already connected. The Buddhist idea is that what we see as reality is in fact illusion: the idea of there being an "I" that is separate from "you" is illusion. There is no "I" and there is no "you": we are all one.

Usui gave his students tools to use to better experience oneness. Most students used meditations or chanted a sacred sound, but for the Imperial Officers a symbol was introduced, and we can use this symbol to experience a state of oneness to help us with our distant healing, which is an important part of the practice of Reiki at Second Degree in the Western tradition.

On the next page you can see a symbol that you can use to help you experience a state of oneness, a symbol that you can use to carry out distant healing and which can also be used when treating someone, if you like. This symbol is different from CKR and SHK because the 'distant healing' symbol does not produce an energy: it does not elicit earth ki, it does not elicit heavenly ki. It elicits a state within the practitioner, a state where you can move beyond time and space.

Because of oneness, when you carry out distant healing you create a oneness or a wholeness within yourself, you heal yourself, and you heal the other person: you are one.

What I am going to do in this section is to introduce you to the 'distant healing' symbol, show you how to draw it and how to say its name, and how to use this symbol when sending Reiki to another person.

The Third Symbol: Hon Sha Ze Sho Nen - Oneness

Pronunciation Guide

Hon   rhymes with 'gone', 'on'
Sha   pronounced like this: 'shah'
Ze   pronounced 'zay', rhymes with
'day', 'hay'
Sho   as in 'show'
Nen   rhymes with 'men', 'when', 'hen'

Even emphasis on all syllables

Drawing Instructions → → → →

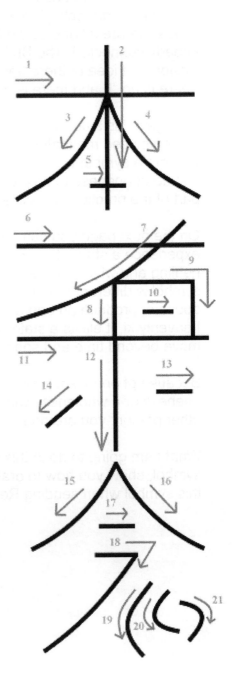

Where did the 'distant healing' symbol come from?

Like CKR and SHK, HonShaZeShoNen (HSZSN) is an existing symbol, or at least it is composed of five existing Japanese kanji that you can find in a Japanese dictionary (see right). It is not completely clear what the meaning of this symbol is, because the component kanji have been 'overlapped' so that they produce one big composite character. For example the bottom part of 'hon' looks like the upper part of 'sha' and so the two are merged to eliminate repetition of the same shapes and lines. The same applies to the bottom part of 'sha' and the top part of 'ze' etc.

Each kanji has a range of meanings that change with context and when combined with other kanji and so there are endless combinations and shades of meaning and interpretation. On a course I attended with Frank Arjava Petter and Chetna Koyabashi, Chetna was not able to say what the symbol meant, for this reason.

In 'secret' Shintoism the phrase 'honshazeshonen' means 'man and God are one', but it is not known how this is written. Hiroshi Doi gives the meaning as 'I unite with God'. One interpretation in the West is to give the meaning 'bring wholeness and completion now'. Another interpretation is 'the light within me reaches out to the light within you (recipient) to promote peace, healing and understanding'.

In any case, HSZSN is not a symbol that produces energy, as are CKR and SHK. HSZSN allows the Reiki energy to be connected in a particular way: in a way where you do not have to worry about time or distance, and it is an integral part of Reiki practice.

HonShaZeShoNen can be used to send healing energy to someone sitting next to you (without putting your hands on them). You can send Reiki to someone who is the other side of the street, in a different village or town, or in a different continent.

Distant Healing works, that is without doubt. It is an integral part of the Reiki system, and it is not a technique that is 'peculiar to Reiki', because it is practised by conventional spiritual healers and other energy workers too.

Approaches to carrying out distant healing

Some people are taught that distant healing is not possible at First Degree level, and that distant healing is only possible once you have been attuned to the distant healing symbol on a Reiki Second Degree course. This is not the case. From the moment that you start practising Reiki at First Degree you can send Reiki at a distance, you do not need to use the 'distant healing' symbol to send distant healing, and you do not need to be 'attuned' to the distant healing symbol for it to work for you. What we do at Second Degree is to introduce a tool that you can use to help your distant healing become perhaps more focused, or we can say that you learn to experience a state of oneness more deeply so that you can click into that state more effortlessly when you send distant healing.

Below I have brought together a range of approaches that you can use to carry out distant healing, some simple, some more complex. You will have realised by now that the detail of the ritual you use is not important and that your underlying intent is the significant thing when using Reiki, whether working on yourself or on another person.

In the same way that Reiki treatments are most effective when carried out on a number of occasions, rather than as a one-off, with distant healing, too, the practice is more effective if the distant healing sessions are repeated. Distant healing does not take anything like as long as hands-on treatments and you should send distant healing for perhaps 10-15 minutes on each occasion, ideally carrying this out each day for 3-5 days, though you can send every day if you like.

Self-Treatment meditation approach

You are familiar with the self-treatment meditation, where you imagine that you are treating a carbon copy of yourself, sitting on the floor in front of you in your mind's eye. Well why not put someone else in front of you in your imagination, and have in mind that energy is flowing into those five areas of the other person's head? You can even use the guided meditation audio track on your CD to guide you through this.

Here is a suitable simple scheme:

1. Close your eyes and take a few long deep breaths
2. Focus your attention on your Tanden point
3. Say to yourself that "this is to be a distant healing for the highest good of …."
4. Imagine the person sitting on the floor in front of you
5. In your mind's eye, imagine or have in mind that energy is flowing into the person's head, in the five positions that you are familiar with

6. When you are ready to bring things to a close, imagine the person disappearing, take a few long deep breaths again, and bring yourself back

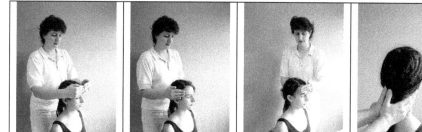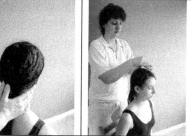

You do not have to be able to see the other person clearly in your mind's eye; you do not need to visualise well at all. It is sufficient to intend that the energy is flowing to particular areas of the head, or allow your attention to rest or to dwell on those areas, whether or not you can 'see' them. The energy will follow your focus and direct itself to where your attention is directed.

If you want receive some feedback from the recipient you will need to agree with them a set time for them to sit down to receive, and for you to send, the distant healing.

We suggest sending distant healing for about 10-15 minutes. The recipient may well be aware of things happening, but this will not always be the case.

An even simpler approach

The details of any ritual used in distant healing are optional, so we can take an even simpler approach. The bare bones of distant healing are to know where you are sending the energy – to set a definite intent – and to allow the energy to flow, so you could try this:

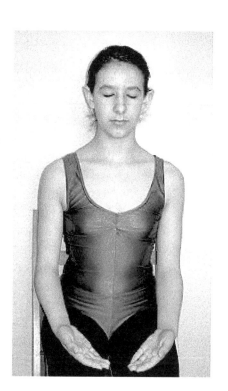

1. Close your eyes and take a few long deep breaths
2. Focus your attention on your Tanden point
3. Say to yourself that "this is to be a distant healing for the highest good of …."
4. Focus your attention on the recipient in your mind's eye
5. Feel yourself merging with the recipient, becoming one with them
6. Allow the energy to flow from you to them for as long as feels appropriate
7. When you are ready to bring things to a close, feel your attention withdrawing from the recipient, take a few long deep breaths again, and bring yourself back

In both of the above examples, we dedicated the distant healing to the recipient's highest good, which means that we were neutral in the process, not directing the energy to achieve a particular thing. We approach distant healing in the same way that we approach treating another person: we have no expectations, we stand aside, we allow the energy to do whatever is appropriate for that person. The energy is drawn through us according to the recipient's need without any interference from us; we have no thought or desire about the outcome.

'Western style" distant healing methods

Distant healing is carried out in a wide variety of ways in different lineages, some methods being more complex than others, and some methods being more dogmatic than others. Some students are taught that if they do not carry out distant healing in a particular way then it will not work for them. This is unhelpful and Reiki is certainly not constrained by the details of man-made rituals.

So there are no hard and fast rules associated with distant healing, other than knowing where the energy is going (setting a definite intent), using HSZSN in some way, and allowing the energy to flow. This lack of certainty can be rather disconcerting for some people, and liberating for others, so you can choose your method according to your taste. So long as you know where you want the energy to go, and use HonShaZeShoNen in some way, then the energy will get there. You will find your own preferred technique.

Remember that no way is better than any other. Some people feel more comfortable with a more detailed ritual, others are content to set a definite intent, use HonShaZeShoNen to make the connection in some way, and they then blank their minds to allow the energy to flow, and visualise no longer. Do what feels right for you.

Here are some methods that people have used successfully:

1. Draw HonShaZeShoNen over a teddy bear or a doll, or a pillow, and Reiki the pillow etc. with the intention that the energy is sent to the recipient
2. Draw HonShaZeShoNen over your upper leg, and Reiki your leg with the intention that it represents the recipient. You knee represents their head and so on.
3. Shrink the recipient in your imagination so that (s)he fits in the palm of your hand, draw HonShaZeShoNen over your hand, cup the other hand over the top and send Reiki through an energy tube to the recipient; blank your mind and just let the energy flow
4. Imagine the person, visualise HonShaZeShoNen over them, and imagine that you are carrying out a Reiki treatment on them, even to the extent of drawing symbols over your imaginary hands if you like

5. As a variation, imagine a door, draw HonShaZeShoNen over the door and imagine it opening to allow Reiki to pass to the recipient

Below I include two detailed descriptions of suggested rituals, but they are just suggestions: do not follow them slavishly, or do not follow them at all!

Distant Healing Method #1: Cupping your hands

Below is a method based on one used by one of my teachers, Diane Whittle. Basically you visualise the recipient and shrink them down so that they fit between your hands. Visualise the distant healing symbol over your hand to make a connection and let the energy flow using either ChoKuRei or SeiHeKi, as required. I like to clear a space on my desk, light a candle and maybe some incense and just sit quietly for a while watching the candle flame and the plume of smoke from the incense stick. It helps me to relax and quieten my mind. It sets the scene for the ritual to follow.

This is what I do next:

1. Settle yourself down and blank your mind for a few moments.
2. Say to yourself that this is to be a distant healing for the highest healing good of _____.
3. Visualise the person (if you know them) and imagine them as they might be in their usual surroundings, home etc. in order to make a connection with them.
4. Imagine the person being shrunk down so that they fit in the palm of your non-dominant hand.
5. Draw HonShaZeShoNen over the palm of your non-dominant hand, visualising the symbol in violet and saying its name three times.
6. Close your other hand over the top so that the person is 'cupped' botwoon your handc.
7. Say to yourself' distant healing… connect' and imagine a tube of energy flowing from your cupped hands to the person you are treating, surrounding and engulfing their entire body with vibrant healing energy.
8. Visualise ChoKuRei or SeiHeKi as required, saying the symbol name three times, and imagine energy derived from that symbol flowing to the person.
9. Alternatively, just let the energy flow as it wants.
10. Perhaps imagine yourself carrying out a brief treatment on the person
11. Perhaps be creative: flood their body with brilliant white light, flushing away any negativity or disease; imagine some psychic surgery, reaching in and removing diseased parts.
12. You do not have to actively visualise; you can just let the Reiki flow.
13. Continue this for about 10-15 minutes
14. Finish by saying to yourself 'I seal this treatment with light and love and universal wisdom'. Intend that the healing effect is sealed in and that the benefits will be long-lasting.
15. Say to yourself 'distant healing… disconnect', visualising the energy tube disconnecting and disappearing.

16. Ritually disconnect as you would normally, rubbing or shaking your hands, blowing through them etc.

"Stacking" HSZSN

HSZSN is quite a long symbol, obviously, and depending on how big you make the symbol, you could find that it stretches way beyond your palm when you draw it. To get around this you can 'stack' the sections of the symbol on top of each other, for example drawing the first seven lines as the first 'layer', then moving your hand back to the 'start' position and drawing the next nine lines, finally moving your hand back to the start one more time, to draw the final five strokes.

Distant Healing Method #2: using your leg as a prop

This technique is one that was taught to me, but it seems a bit cumbersome, and I don't get on with it very well. It uses your leg as a substitute for the recipient of the healing, and some people like it! Why not give it a try.

You can use other substitutes, like a doll or a teddy bear or a pillow, but they are not essential: they are merely props to focus your intent. Things do not have to be complicated.

Follow these steps...

1. Sit down in front of the table with the picture on it.
2. Place your hands together in prayer, ground and centre yourself: take a few deep breaths and blank your mind.
3. Connect the ether tube: Draw HonShaZeShoNen with the dominant hand, visualising the symbol in violet and saying the symbol name three times.
4. Say out loud 'I wish this healing to be connected to (the person's name and location)'.
5. Your upper legs represent the recipient's body. Work on your legs:
6. Your left leg represents the back of their body
7. Your right leg represents the front of their body
8. Your knees represent their head and your groin represents their feet
9. Draw ChoKuRei over the problem area of your leg with palm down, fingers together. Visualise in violet and say the symbol name silently three times.
10. Draw SeiHeKi over your knee (representing the recipient's head) if emotional balancing is needed.
11. Contract your Huiyin (see p.84) and put your tongue to the roof of your mouth.
12. Place your left hand over each problem area with your right hand over the left, and perpendicular to it.
13. Move your hands to various positions as necessary. Move your hands when the warmth or flow of energy stops.

14. When you are finished, say out loud ' I wish this effort to be used for the wellbeing of all entities everywhere'.

If you have difficulty in visualising your legs as a body, it has been suggested that you can draw on an old pair of trousers so you know where to place your hands!

Using CKR and SHK when sending distant healing

If you wish you can use CKR or SHK when carrying out distant healing. If you had a strong feeling or impression that one energy or the other was required then, having made the 'connection' to the recipient, you could have in mind the symbol of CKR or SHk and imagine that this energy was flowing to the recipient.

But most people who send distant healing will just send 'Reiki' and allow the energy to do what it needs. It is best to keep things simple.

Using Distant Healing creatively

People have developed many creative ways of working with and focusing distant healing. Typically, you use it to send healing to someone who is not close enough to touch, but because distant healing works outside of time and space, people have also sent 'distant' Reiki to:

1. Yourself as a child, your inner child, difficult episodes in your past
2. Yourself in the future, in an anticipated difficult situation (e.g. a job interview)
3. Your past life/lives, or future life/lives
4. Someone who has 'passed on'
5. Heal a relationship between two people, but always for 'the highest good'.
6. Global crises, e.g. the Gulf War, the Kosovo crisis, families and victims of 9/11
7. The planet earth, nature, your garden
8. Divine figures, e.g. Buddha, Jesus, Krishna, the Goddess, Jehovah

Heal your Past

Reiki can be sent to your past, to deal with bad situations in your past that have really left their mark – e.g. a bad argument with a family member, or an event, that has produced effects that ripple down the years. By imagining the situation and sending distant Reiki to it, you are dealing with and healing the effect that the situation has on you now in terms of the way you think and feel about what happened. You are healing the effect that it has had on your emotions, and the way that you interpret what happened. You are not sending

Reiki 'back in time'. All you have is now and that is when the energy produces its effects.

You can imagine yourself in a childlike state to 'heal the inner child'.

Send Reiki to the Future

Reiki can be sent to your future, for example a public speaking engagement or job interview, intending that you will be flooded with Reiki when you get there.

People who believe in reincarnation, or perhaps some knowledge of past lives, can send Reiki to their past lives, or even future lives!

Try an experiment

Try this experiment on another Reiki person, or another willing volunteer – particularly if they are quite sensitive to the energy: for one week, send distant healing at 10pm, or whatever time you agree upon with the other person. The recipient should lay quietly with no distractions and be aware of any sensations they experience. See what happens:

1. For some days, send Reiki at the agreed time.
2. For some days, don't send the energy at all!
3. For some days, send the energy earlier on, and 'intend' that it will go out later.

Distant Healing Books

Send distant healing to multiple recipients by having a 'distant healing book'. Write down a list of names in the book, review the list before you start, draw HSZSN over the book and then channel Reiki into the book with the intention that it will be sent to everyone in the book.

Reiki will still work even if you do not know the recipient, so there are distant healing 'networks' that will send Reiki to any names supplied to them. Although you may not know who the person is, the person who asked for the healing knows them, and that connection is sufficient for the energy to reach the right target.

Distant Healing Boxes

Alternatively, use a 'distant healing box' containing pieces of paper with names written on them, photographs etc. Draw HSZSN over the box and

Reiki the box with the intention that the energy will be sent out to everyone represented inside it.

Reiki Your Day

Send Reiki to your day using HonShaZeShoNen. I know a lady who does this, and she finds that the hours seem to expand to allow her to get through everything she needs to do. If she does not get everything done, she does not worry too much about it!

Reiki Your Bed

Another lady sends Reiki to her bed, with the intention that the energy will wait there for her, and flow into her when she gets into bed at night. You can send Reiki to the future in an 'unconditional' form: it doesn't have to be set to be released at 10.00pm GMT... it can be sent with the intention that the energy will be released when a certain thing happens. E.g. when you walk into an interview room. Thus you don't have to worry about Reiki landing on the previous candidate if things end up running late!

Some Case Histories

Alison

Alison was doing distant healing on her mother, who sat down at the pre-agreed time in a quiet place. She noticed the sudden appearance of coloured lights - mostly blue - which abruptly stopped a while later. The time on the clock when the light show stopped was the time when Alison stopped sending Reiki.

Alison usually does distant healing by imagining that she is doing a Reiki treatment on the person - only at a distance. Her mother, when on the receiving end of this, has felt heat and tingling moving from one part of her body to another, in line with Alison's intention.

Suzanne

Suzanne was doing some distant healing on her Grandmother on a number of consecutive evenings at an agreed time, and her Grandmother was definitely experiencing something distinctive at the agreed moment.

On one day of the week, however, Suzanne was going to be out in the evening, so she sent Reiki out at lunchtime with the intention that the energy would be received at the prearranged time. On that evening her Grandmother experienced the same sensations as she had on the previous evenings.

Megan

Megan is one of my daughters who, in April 2000 (then aged 7), was knocked over by a car. She ended up in Hospital for 8 days and had a 3-hour operation to put all the facial bones back in the right place - the accident caved in the side of her face. Shortly after the accident happened I posted an e-mail message on a Reiki discussion group on the Internet, asking for people to send distant Reiki, and within a day I had received 50 e-mails from people all over the country. One lady suggested that everyone got together at 10pm to send one big lot of Reiki each night.

My wife Lorraine, who stayed in Hospital with Megan all the time, did not know that this was going on.

One evening Lorraine sat down on the bed next to Megan, ready to start doing some Reiki on her face, when she was amazed to feel a sort of electric fizzing or tingling, and a huge amount of heat radiating off Megan. Lorraine said "you could almost see the energy coming off the top of her head". This happened at 10.05pm, five minutes after the big distant healing session started. Megan was a little Reiki radiator!

When I told Megan that lots of people were sending Reiki to her, she said "that's why I can see all those blue lights in my head", which is what she normally experiences when on the receiving end of distant Reiki.

Megan coped very well with all the painful things that were done to her, and recovered from her two doses of anaesthetic very quickly indeed. Reiki was very useful to us because it gave us something that we could do to help, rather than just sitting there. For example, the effects of her intravenous morphine would wear off after a while, and Reiki stopped the pain, tiding her over until the next dose of painkiller was due.

Lorraine and I were also on the receiving end of distant healing, and this helped Megan because we were able to cope with and deal with the things that were going on around us in a positive way.

The Ethics of Distant Healing

Some people are of the opinion that it is totally unethical to send distant Reiki to a person if they have not given their permission first. They see it as a gross intrusion, interference, a violation of that person's personal space, a violation of their energy field.

I do not agree with this point of view.

On the basis that:

1. Reiki is a beautiful healing energy that will not cause anyone any harm.

2. Any Reiki sent is dedicated to the 'highest good' of the recipient, so that it is line with their karma or destiny. This means that you are not manipulating them or imposing your preferred result on the situation.
3. If the person really does not want to be healed, then the Reiki will not work.
4. You do not obtain someone's permission if you are going to pray for them, and I see sending distant healing rather like a concentrated form of prayer, where you are asking for Divine intervention in someone's life, in whatever way is appropriate for them.

… then I see no problem in sending Reiki to whoever you want to. If someone was lying in the road, unconscious after a road accident, would you refrain from sending Reiki just because they couldn't sit up and give you consent in writing? Scare stories about people being made to wake up when under an anaesthetic when receiving distant Reiki, or falling asleep at the wheel of a car, are just nonsense as far as I am concerned. If you are really worried that this might happen, then simply intend that the energy be received by the person at whatever moment is appropriate for them in the next 24 hours.

We should remind ourselves that when we send distant Reiki we are neutral in the process, we have no expectations and we do not push for a particular outcome. We stand aside and what the energy does, if anything, is out of our hands. We offer the energy to the recipient; we do not force it on them.

Distant Space Clearing

You now know that ChoKuRei can be used for space clearing. You know that Reiki can be sent at a distance… well, it is possible to do distant space clearing, too. This had not actually occurred to me, until one of my Reiki 2 students mentioned that she was doing it, with quite some success it seems. What Joy does is to take a floor-plan of the house to be cleared, showing the doors and windows. She calls on Mikao Usui, Mrs Takata and the ascended Masters to keep her safe and help her in her endeavours. She then imagines that she is moving through each room, drawing ChoKuRei over the walls, ceiling and floor, and flooding the room with light/Reiki.

She gave an example of a little girl who hated being in her bedroom, and would not go to bed there happily. The day after Joy did the space-clearing, the little girl trotted up to bed without any problem.

Why not give it a try and see what you notice.

Finding your own style

Here I want to include some distant healing methods that are used by some of my students, to demonstrate that you can find your own individual style. As you can see, the have found their own special way with the energy...

"I have a book with all the names in. I read through all the names first and try visualising any of the people I know, but aside from that I just hold the book between my hands and intend the energy to go to everyone in the book. I'm confident that the energy does follow my intention. I remember after the 2nd degree course, at first I would be quite slow drawing the symbols and I quickly noticed that I was tuned into the energy I was intending before I had finished drawing the symbol or saying its name."
Tina

"I usually burn some incense, light a candle, put on relaxing music and after I do my Hatsurei I draw my symbol on hands and visualise drawing it above my head. I turn on Reiki and ask for the healing to be sent to all the names and situations written in my healing box, that healing be sent out to all at 10.00pm every night of the week, when all healing goes out. I also add any other things that may need Reiki e.g. a dance we may be performing etc. I sit there and let the Reiki flow for about 10 minutes in which I usually end up in an altered state of consciousness. I could stay there all day!"
Laetitia

"I realised I have no set procedure when I'm sending distant healing. Sometimes after Hatsurei and a Self-treatment I send Reiki to the list of people on my scrap of paper. I send Reiki energy and love and light and the highest healing good to all the names. I say every person's name three times and after if there is anyone on the list that I know personally then I visualise them and visualise sending Reiki to the parts of that person that need it. Sometimes throughout the day I think about someone on the list quite out of the blue and tune in and send them healing. I feel distant healing is personal but at the same time universal."
Natalie

"I use several different methods depending on the circumstances. For my distant healing list I have a little photo album with pictures of people and a list of names. I spend a little time looking through the book and then send the Reiki.

"My grandmother has my favourite quartz crystal point. I send Reiki to reside in the point so any time she is in pain she can hold it and then the Reiki flows to her.

"Sending to a specific person for a specific reason I will spend a little time picturing their face and turn to face them geographically. I then visualise waves of healing energy flowing in their direction and reaching the point where it's needed."
David

"When I first began I remember setting up some kind of sacred hospital room, with 'patients' lying in beds, which I'd visit one after the other, treating each one. This became too cumbersome, and I abandoned the elaborate visualising.

"But it's not silly to visualise things, after all. My son recently asked me to send him healing for a rash on his back. I visualised a pot of paint, over which I made CKR, and visualised the paint as violet. Then I painted his back.

"Sometimes I just let the image of the person rest in my mind and then let whatever I'm led to do happen. Accompanying this are often other images.

"When I send out healing last thing at night I do Hatsurei and then put one clear unpolished quartz piece into each hand, cup my hands together, and then send out healing to each person individually.

"In the mornings I've taken to using a lovely box, in which I've put slips of paper for each healing, and I just sit with the box in my charged hands, running over the names and intentions of each person (or event) in the box. I sit and wait until the buzzing in my hands stops."
Robert

Students' experiences of carrying out distant healing

"You should advise more people who can't do Reiki shares to use the mailing list for DH help. I had the best feedback from some of the list members. Thanks for suggesting it. I feel much more confident about my ability to send DH, and my own perceptions in receiving Reiki (DH sent by two of the women who worked with me from the list)."
Karen Small, USA

"I have carried out distant healing treatments on 4 people always at the same pre-arranged time.

"1st person: she felt like her legs and arms were getting heavier and heavier but as the same time felt like she was on a "cloud". Also told

me she fell asleep straight away after the 10 minutes. This person has eyes and a toe condition, the pain has gone after a few treatments and she is still OK at the moment.

"2nd person : she felt very relaxed, had a little bit of pain in the chest during the session and again fell asleep after 10 minutes, suffering from 2 major conditions, the feel good effect does not seem to last long but she managed to sleep very well and more alert during the days after the sessions.

"3rd person : she was feeling a bit of pain in the lower back during the sessions and heaviness. Also had tingling sensations. She had been suffering from a bad back problem for a few days and told me that after the treatments she could sleep better and move more easily. Also the pain has gone since yesterday.

"4th person : he is my friend I have mentioned previously who is HIV+. He has felt a strong warm sensation and tingling during the treatments, also heaviness in the arms and legs. He has been sleeping properly and had more energy in the day, being able to do more than usual. "
Bruno Cassani, Essex

"The distance healing is going well and I've had some great feedback. Both parents have felt warm tingly sensations at the appropriate times and my friend Angie has been sleeping like a log even though she is sitting exams. She has felt a warm energy type sensation throughout her body...........she hasn't had the tingly feeling but she doesn't get this whilst I treat her anyway.

"All of them had no sensations when I didn't send the energy too and the book seems to be the most favourite way of sending the energy."
Niki Leach, Tyne & Wear

"I've tried the various techniques of distance healing, and so far am most comfortable with a variation on the self-treatment method, visualizing the recipient in front of me and me healing them – that was very powerful and I felt a lot. It also gave me a chance to experiment with the two symbols as well as with the distance healing symbol. The results from it were a bit mixed; the people I was sending to happened to be preoccupied with other things in their lives on the pre-arranged days for me sending it.

"I was also happy with the distance healing book, in which I write people's names and heal them via the book. I like the idea of it, and also time-wise it is far better for me. I feel a lot whilst doing it this way. I connect to Reiki, say that this is a distance healing session for x, y & z, read through the names of the people, visualizing them, draw the HSZSN symbol over the book, then place my hands over the book and, in your own words, just let the energy flow.

"One thing I've noticed over the past weeks is the intensity of Reiki seems to have increased a great deal, and that has felt really nice."
Jason Brown, Wales

"I have also done some distance healing with my brother in France and my sister who lives only five miles away. My brother was very positive and very convinced that the energy had contributed to the healing of a knee problem that he had. He is a builder and had injured it while building a swimming pool. He swears it could feel it tingling when he sat down at the agreed time and I sent the healing.

"...Having just got back from France I have been sending distance Reiki on a regular basis to a couple of people, one of whom has recently experienced a very traumatic relationship breakdown and has professed himself very grateful for the peace that Reiki has given him, allowing him to cope much more successfully than he thought possible. I do not always tell him when I am sending the Reiki but he always seems to know anyway which is very gratifying!"
Gill Oliver, Surrey

Working on Other People

Since you are following a Reiki Second Degree course you will already be comfortable with treating people. You will probably have done 'short blasts' on people's painful knees or shoulders or backs, you will probably have done some 'head and shoulders' treatments on people sitting in a straight-backed chair, and you will have carried out some 'full' Reiki treatments with the recipient supine, starting with the shoulders, treating the head and shoulders, and then moving on to treat the torso and legs.

You will have learned some 'standard' hand positions to use when treating people and you will have followed a simple treatment approach that can be summarised by these few words:

1. Affirm
2. Connect
3. Build
4. Merge
5. Flow

Just as a reminder, here is the basic scheme that you followed when carrying out a full treatment on someone:

1. Close your eyes and bring your hands into the prayer position
2. Take a few long deep breaths to still your mind
3. Remind your self that you are neutral in the process – **Affirm** that the treatment is for the 'highest good' of the recipient.
4. Imagine energy/light passing down to you from above, flowing through your crown down to your Tanden: **Connect**
5. Imagine/feel the energy building up in your Tanden; we work from the Tanden: **Build**
6. Spend some time feeling the recipient's energy field
7. Spend some time 'scanning' the body
8. Rest your hands on the recipient's shoulders
9. Feel yourself merging with the energy and with the recipient: **Merge**
10. Allow the energy to flow, and move on to other hand positions when ready: **Flow**

You already know that the treatment of others was not the main thrust of Usui Sensei's system, there were no treatment techniques taught, and his approach to treating other people, such as it was, involved the use of intuition to determine any hand placements. Also, the energies of earth ki and heavenly ki that were introduced to Second Degree students, for reasons of self-healing and spiritual development, could be used to treat others. So the ways in which your treatments will change at Second Degree are as follows:

1. You can use the Reiki symbols when you treat
2. You will learn how to place your hands intuitively rather than following a standard set of hand positions

In the following paragraphs I will explain how to use CKR, SHK and HSZSN when treating people, I will explain how to approach working intuitively, using a Japanese method called 'Reiji ho', and I will talk more about the importance of intent. In the Appendix you can read about a whole range of ways in which the Reiki symbols are used in Western Reiki; none of these methods having anything to do with the system that Usui Sensei was teaching. They are included for your information.

Using CKR and SHK when you treat

The first thing to say is that you are not obliged to use the Reiki symbols to treat people, but doing so can enhance the effects of the treatments, making them more intense and beneficial for the recipient. Using CKR or SHK when you treat someone has the effect of boosting the flow of energy and flooding the recipient with the energy of earth ki or heavenly ki; this will have powerful effects at the physical level, or at the mental/emotional level. You can use the symbols in each hand position, in some of the hand positions, or in none of the hand positions.

How to Draw CKR and SHK when you treat

When you used the Reiki symbols for meditation, this is what you did:

- You imagined the symbol by drawing it out in your mind's eye, seeing the symbol being traced as if it was being drawn by hand with a pen or brush
- You imagined the symbol being traced in violet if you could visualise colours
- Then you said the symbol's name silently to yourself, three times, like a mantra

The use of the Reiki symbols when treating other people is similar in that you are going to trace or visualise the symbol and you are going to say the symbol's name to yourself, silently, three times. When you are treating someone you can draw the symbol out using your fingers and thumb coned together, if you like. Here are some variations you can use:

- With one hand resting on the recipient, use your other hand to draw a symbol in the air above the back of your hand, and as you say the name silently to yourself three times, 'tap' the air: tap, tap, tap. The 'tapping' is optional but many people do this. Imagine the symbol passing through your hand into the recipient.

- If you are using both hands to treat, for example the temples or the heart or the knee, draw the symbol using an imaginary 'very long nose' (like Pinocchio or Cyrano de Bergerac), and use small head movements to trace the symbol over your hands or over the part of the body where the energy is being directed (for example, treat the temples and visualise the symbol over the part of the head that is between your hands).
- Just use eye movements to trace out the symbol over your hand or hands or over a part of the recipient's body.
- You can draw the symbol in your mind's eye, or – with practice – visualise the symbol over your hand etc. in its entirety.
- Incidentally, you can 'tap' the symbol you have drawn, using your 'nose' or 'eyes', or your intent!

In all the above examples you are making some sort of a direct connection between the symbol and either your hand (or hands) or the part of the body where the energy is being directed. What you do not do is to treat the temples and visualise CKR over someone's ankle.

If you like you could draw out the symbol again in that same hand position, but do not go overboard. Sometimes drawing the symbol more than once can help to increase the flow of energy a bit more, but drawing the symbol more than three times is a waste of time.

When you move into a new hand position you will need to renew your connection to a particular energy by drawing out the symbol again.

We recommend this approach to using CKR and SHK when treating

The most elegant and simple way of using CKR or SHK when you treat is to follow the instructions below. This approach uses no hand movements, no head movements, no 'tapping' and is more of a meditative practice than a 'technique'. When you meditated on CKR and SHK you visualised a great big CKR, for example, up in the air above you (representing the source of the energy), you said the symbol's name silently to yourself three times to 'empower' it, and you imagined that energy or light was cascading down to you from the symbol. We can use a variation of this method when treating someone else:

1. Visualise, say, SHK up in the air above you and say the symbol's name three times silently to yourself to 'empower' the symbol.
2. Draw energy down from the symbol. The energy passes through your crown, down the centre of your body to your Tanden, building in your Tanden.
3. Have in mind that this energy is flooding down to you, and through your hands into the recipient.

4. If you feel you need to, occasionally 'renew' the symbol by visualising it again and saying its name three times silently to yourself. Do not go overboard with this.

As you move from one hand position to another, you do not need to keep on redrawing the symbol if you are still using the same energy: just leave the symbol up there (you have already put it there even if it has disappeared from your mind's eye) and keep on allowing the energy to flow from it. You are likely to just 'drift' as you treat, empty and still. You don't need to see the symbol in your mind's eye clearly all the time: you put it there, you set a definite intent, and that is usually sufficient.

To stop channelling that particular energy strongly then just have in mind that the symbol has disintegrated and disappeared. To emphasise the energy of the other symbol, dissolve the earlier symbol and visualise the new symbol above you, and repeat the above sequence.

How do I decide what symbol to use, if any, when I treat?

Ideally, you will allow your intuition to guide you in terms of what aspect of the energy you emphasise – if any – as you carry out your treatment. This will come with time and practice. In the meantime, though, and on the basis that the energy of CKR focuses the energy on physical healing and the energy of SHK produces mental/emotional balancing or release, you could:

1. Use SHK on the head, heart and solar plexus – areas where thoughts and emotions reside (in the head, and in the heart and solar plexus chakras)
2. Use CKR elsewhere, or in fact anywhere on the body

So using SHK on the head could deal with a busy mind, and using it on the heart and solar plexus could encourage an emotional release. CKR could be used on an arthritis knee, or a sports injury or a bad back.

This general 'rule of thumb' comes with the proviso that if you have a feeling that you should use a particular symbol in a particular area, you should go with that feeling or impression whether or not it makes 'sense'. You know from the First Degree course that your thoughts end emotions are not just held in your head and your heart, so if you feel you need to use SHK on someone's knee then just do it. You don't need to understand why. Go with your impressions and feelings, accept them uncritically and act upon them.

Should I mix the energies of CKR and SHK when treating?

This is not a good idea. Doing this will do something, but it is far more effective in practice to use the energies individually, not mixed up. Your meditations on the energies of CKR and SHK will have demonstrated to you that these energies are very, very different, like chalk and cheese, and it is far better to keep your practice simple. Emphasise earth ki or heavenly ki, or neither, as you move from one hand position to another.

Western Reiki has complicated things further by introducing such things as 'symbol sandwiches' where you draw out one symbol, and then put another symbol on top of it, and then another, and so on, or there is also the idea that you should draw CKR on top of other symbols always, on the basis that it is some sort of 'power' symbol. This is a very un-Japanese approach, has no basis in what Mikao Usui was teaching, and is supremely unhelpful. This is a cluttered and confused Reiki practice which has nothing to commend it and should be avoided.

Using only one symbol during a treatment

If you were to channel energy from only one symbol during an entire treatment, the treatment would be quite intense. Because you are not chopping or changing from one energy to another, the energy seems to have the opportunity to penetrate quite deeply. What makes this technique special is that the body is allowed to resonate at a single frequency for an entire treatment, and the longer that the person is resonating at that frequency, the better. So you would put the chosen symbol up in the air, representing the source of energy, say its name three times silently to yourself, and you go through the treatment, renewing the symbol if you feel prompted to.

If a person's main problem is a mental one (stress for example) or an emotional one, then you could choose to do one or two treatments using SHK on its own, channelling this energy into all hand positions throughout the course of the whole treatment. If a person's main problem is physical, you could choose to do some of the treatments using CKR alone, uninterrupted.

If you are going to carry out a course of treatments, perhaps you might choose to carry out the first treatment without using symbols, by way of providing them with more of a gentle 'introductory' treatment, and then on subsequent sessions you could introduce the symbols, either using both symbols during the course of the subsequent treatments, or perhaps using just one symbol during a treatment if that felt the right thing to do. This is not a hard and fast rule, just a suggestion. Go with what feels appropriate.

How will the CKR and SHK energies feel when I treat someone?

Most people can feel a definite difference between the two energies when meditating on CKR and SHK, and many people can feel a difference in the two energies when they are flowing through your hands into the recipient. The sensations and impressions you have of earth ki and heavenly ki will be felt in your hands and may also be felt within your body, and will tend to echo your experience when meditating on these symbols.

So you will probably feel CKR energy as being heavy, thick, solid, and coarse, like treacle. This is because CKR reduces the frequency of the energy you are channelling to a low level, suitable for healing the physical body (if we are thinking in terms of the 'frequency model'), and because you feel things with your physical body then the effects of CKR are most easily noticeable to you.

By contrast, you are likely to feel SHK energy as being light, delicate, fine or wispy. This is because SHK produces energy at a higher frequency than CKR (if we are thinking in terms of the 'frequency model'), an energy more suitable for healing the mental and emotional aspects of a person. Because SHK vibrates at a higher 'frequency' than the physical body, the effects of this symbol are less easy to discern, though it is no less powerful than CKR.

What will the recipient feel when treated with CKR and SHK?

Most people that you treat will not be able to feel any difference in the quality of the energy when you use a symbol or change from one symbol to another: they will just feel 'Reiki' – heat from your hands, commonly. A few people may feel a difference and this is more likely if they have already been attuned to Reiki, which sensitises people to such things.

If the recipient feels a difference between the two energies, their experience is likely to echo the descriptions given above, though everyone is different and occasionally the recipient (and the practitioner for that matter) can experience the energies in 'non-standard' ways. There is no 'correct' way to experience the energies of CKR and SHK. Many people have similar experiences, but different experiences are not wrong, just different. All we have is out own experience; how could that be wrong? We experience the energies in the way that we experience them. The experience of others may be different.

Students' experiences of using CKR and SHK to treat others

"Channelling energy using CKR and SHK: I did this exercise on my family. I felt the energy differences in my hands. My family didn't seem to notice big differences between the two energies. I'll try to see if I can make guinea pigs of my friends now that I'm back home. I was disappointed that I didn't get much response from my family about the energies.

"...With CKR, he felt heat and had some visual sensations (particularly when I was at the heart and solar plexus). He also had sensations of drawing energy into himself. I also tried using the opening foot chakra technique and he really noticed an energizing from that. I felt a strong flow of energy throughout the treatment.

"With SHK, he felt a strong pulse while I worked at his head. Otherwise he didn't notice too much. I felt a strong flow of energy, particularly in his heart and solar plexus and head. The sensations decreased in the rest of his body. The neatest thing was that while I was treating the back of his head, I had a strong image of a boy come into my head. When I mentioned this to Andy later, he said he'd been picturing our son at that time. "
Karen Small, USA

"While my aunty was visiting this week, i have perform a few treatments on her. She had bad sciatica and could hardly move or walk. I have used Chokurei during the treatment and the feeling in my hands was very strong, almost uncomfortable. She is now feeling much better, the pain has gone."
Bruno Cassani, Essex

"My mother in law experienced very strong sensations with CKR as opposed to the normal Reiki, she definitely felt a big difference. A friend who hasn't had it done said my hands were red hot as did the treatment and felt like she was floating on air when I had finished.

"…I did a full treatment on my mother in law and my friend using both the energies and both of them noticed the change even with out telling them when I have been changing them!

"My hand s get a lot more tingly with CKR than with SHK and the flow of energy seems to be a lot stronger too, although with SHK my hands seems to get very, very hot instead."
Niki Leach, Tyne & Wear

"The CKR and SHK treatments went very well, very relaxing for both myself and the recipients as usual, with one CKR recipient comatose in less than a minute! Occasionally I could feel the energy change in some areas even though I had channelled one particular energy, so I just noted this and carried on with the treatment."
Deborah Hartley, London

Using HSZSN when you treat

HSZSN does not produce or elicit an energy. It allows you to experience a state of oneness. Distant healing is an expression of oneness, and treating someone is an expression of oneness too, so you have already experienced this state to an extent, whenever you work on someone.

You can use HSZSN in a limited fashion when you treat someone, and here are a few suggestions:

- Perhaps when you start a treatment, and you are resting your hands on someone's shoulders, you might visualise HSZSN in your mind's eye, superimposing it over the recipient's body, and say its name three times, by way of 'connecting' with the person on all levels, or on a deep level.

- The notion of oneness implies a connecting of 'disconnected' parts, so perhaps you might think about using this symbol when you can see that someone is resisting an emotional release. Visualise HSZSN over the solar plexus so that the emotions are 'connected' and to their exit route and allowed to be released.

- Maybe if you feel that a person needs to express their emotions or their thoughts better, visualise HSZSN over the throat-heart-solar plexus, or throat-head, to 'connect' the mental or emotional areas with the communication centre. This need only be done for a few moments; you are not channelling energy in the way that you are with CKR and SHK.

Do not do these latter two examples in a calculated, planned, analytical fashion. Go with the flow and use the symbol when it feels appropriate. Be guided by your feelings and impressions. You are not here to prescribe or impose a solution: you are more effective as a channel when you are a bystander in the process, using a symbol only when you feel strongly guided to.

You need not use HSZSN at all in a treatment context, and your treatments will still be perfectly effective.

Working with Intuition

Usui Sensei's approach to treating people was based on intuition, and it seems that his students had no problem in working in this way if they treated others. He taught a few standard hand positions - to use on the head - to some of his students, and the rest used intuition for all hand placements.

You may have found that you are working intuitively to a greater or lesser extent already. Maybe when you have been treating people you have felt strangely drawn to a particular area of the body, or perhaps you have even noticed that your hands have wanted to drift to a particular area. This is your intuition starting to come through.

Everyone is intuitive. You already know exactly where to put your hands for each person you treat, based on their individual energy needs. But your conscious mind sits there like a big useless lump, preventing you from gaining access to the intuitive knowledge that is already there within you! To help us still our mind and allow our intuition to filter through to the surface, we can use an intuitive approach called 'Reiji ho' which is used in Japanese-style Reiki, and this method has been used in the Usui Reiki Ryoho Gakkai. Reiji ho means 'indication of the spirit technique' – the energy telling you where to treat.

We don't know whether Usui Sensei taught Reiji ho. Most of his students didn't have any problem with working intuitively. But perhaps Usui taught Reiji ho to the Imperial Officers, and this method then continued in the memorial Society that they set up. Who knows? In any case, Reiji ho is an excellent method to allow intuitive working when treating other people and it has allowed hundreds of my students to work intuitively without too many problems.

What happens when you practise Reiji ho is that your hands will drift to areas of need, as if they were being pulled by invisible magnets. Of course it is you who is moving your hands: your brain sending messages to your nerves, you controlling your muscles. But it is the subconscious part of your mind that is controlling the hand movements. So Reiji ho is a bit like dowsing, where the pendulum moves in circles, or up and down, because you are jiggling it, with your subconscious mind controlling the movements. A pendulum is a tool to allow you to access intuitive knowledge, and so is Reiji ho.

When you practise Reiji ho you will be standing by the treatment table and hovering your hands motionless a few inches above the recipient. After a while they should drift and stop. Wherever they stop, you then rest your hands down to treat (obviously depending where they stopped: there are some areas of the body where it would not be appropriate to rest your hands). When you feel that you should move on to another hand position, you bring your hands back to hover over the body, and see where they want to go next. So you do not change the way that you treat, to only hover over the body: you use Reiji ho to work out where to put your hands down to treat.

Sometimes you hands will not necessarily move and stop, but will drift up and down the body for a while, in which case you accept this and allow it to happen. Occasionally one hand will come to a halt and one hand will continue to move for a while. Occasionally your hands will drift further away from the body, so that you are being directed to channel energy into one of the layers of the aura, and after a while your hands should move closer to the body again. Quite often the hand positions will be asymmetrical. There are many variations.

You are likely to end up with fewer hand positions when compared with a standard scheme, each set of positions are likely to be held for longer, and you are likely to feel a great deal of energy coming through: intuitive treatments are usually powerful, more powerful than treatments based on standard hand positions. This makes sense, because you are putting your hands into just the right combination of positions for each person on each occasion. Not only are you putting your hands in just the right places for each recipient that you treat, but you are also directing the energy into the best sequence of positions for each recipient on each occasion. Treatments based on standard sequences of hand positions work well, but intuitively guided treatments are something special.

How I use Reiji ho in practice is to start my treatments by resting my hands on the shoulders for perhaps 10 minutes, as in the 'standard' full treatment; then I allow my hands to drift while treating the head and shoulders; then I move on to the torso and work intuitively there. So I still follow a standard procedure to an extent. It is good to start the treatment by resting your hands on the shoulders because it gets the energy flowing, it helps to still your mind, and it helps to relax the recipient; then moving on to work intuitively on the head, I find that intuition tends to lead you to use non-standard and non-symmetrical hand positions, for example the temples on one side and the front of the face on the other, or over the crown on one side and by the throat on the other; moving on to the torso, I then allow the energy to guide me to wherever it wants to go, sometimes the hand positions are close together, sometimes they are far apart, sometimes there are very few positions and you are 'locked' into one set of hand positions for a long time. I then tend to finish with the ankles, though this is not essential.

How to perform Reiji ho

Reiji ho is very simple: there is no magic formula, really, other than deliberately making yourself open and receptive. You have already started to do this. When you treat someone you empty your mind, merge with the energy, merge with the recipient and allow the energy to flow. Reiji ho continues this practice: you are empty; you have no expectations; you are in neutral; you feel yourself disappearing into the energy, merging with the energy, becoming one with the energy; you allow your hands to drift.

The more you try hard to make Reiji ho work, the less likely it is that it will work. Reiji ho will work for you when you give up and stop trying, stop thinking, stop noticing what is going on in your hands, stop analysing and rationalising. Give up and stop trying and just be with the energy, and Reiji ho will work for you.

With practice it gets easier and easier to click into a lovely, empty, merged state, and after a while your intuitive working will be effortless. This should now be the way that you approach treatments: seated treatments and full treatments.

Here are some suitable instructions:

1. Place your hands in the prayer position, close your eyes, and feel your connection with Reiki through the crown of your head. Take a few long deep breaths.
2. Feel the energy building in your Tanden. We work from the Tanden, the centre of our intuition.
3. Move your hands in front of your third eye, and ask the Reiki energy to guide your hands, to guide your hands to where the energy is needed most. Say to yourself something like 'please let me be guided' or 'please let my hands be guided', 'show me where to treat'.
4. Blank your mind and move your hands down to hover over the recipient.

5. Become one with the energy, join with the energy, merge with the energy that is flowing through your crown, shoulders, arms and hands. Allow your hands to drift.

In fact you do not need to put your hands in the prayer position, nor place them in front of your third eye (a little ritual for connecting your hands to the third eye, which is seen as the chakra associated with intuition). You do not need to say a form of words either. A simpler approach would be as follows:

1. Hover your hands over the recipient and take a few long deep breaths.
2. Feel your connection with Reiki through the crown of your head.
3. Feel the energy building in your Tanden. We work from the Tanden, the centre of our intuition.
4. Blank your mind. Become one with the energy, join with the energy, merge with the energy that is flowing through your crown, shoulders, arms and hands. Allow your hands to drift.

Trying too hard?

To illustrate the need to not try hard when using Reiji ho, I am going to tell you a story about a course I ran in Cumbria a few years ago. The course was an 'update' course for Reiki people at Second Degree or Master level, where I was teaching the methods from Japan. I have taught this course all over the UK and in Europe too. There were about 15-20 people on the course (I can't recall exactly how many) and we were practising Reiji ho on a Saturday afternoon. We had a number of treatment tables set up and there were 3-4 people to each table: one person was on the treatment couch and the other stood around the table practising allowing the energy to guide their hands. They all took turns on the table so everyone had the opportunity to practise Reiji ho on a few different people.

Reiji ho seemed to be working well for everyone except one poor girl whose hands were motionless, and remained motionless no matter how hard she tried to make Reiji ho work. Of course it was her attempts to force Reiji ho to work which were preventing her from achieving success with this method. What I did was to come and stand behind her and rest my hands on her shoulders. Within a minute her hands started to drift. This is not because I was giving her some sort of 'energy boost' but because she was starting to have a bit of a Reiki treatment, and you know the feeling of melting and drifting and relaxing that this can bring within seconds. After a few moments she didn't care what was happening with her hands, she gave up trying, drifted with the treatment – with the energy – and her hands began to drift.

Having proved to herself that she could actually do this, she then went on to make Reiji ho work for her several times; she made it work by not making it work, by giving up and not trying, by just being, in neutral, merged and empty.

Everyone can succeed with this method, but it can be easier for some people than others to give up and stop trying. As soon as you stop trying this method will work for you.

Practical Aspects of Reiji ho

The important thing with both of these versions of Reiji ho is to hold your hands motionless and to hover them. You should not move them deliberately. If you consciously or deliberately move your hands when carrying out Reiji ho, you will override all the subtle sensations and the technique will not work. You should start to notice that your hands want to drift, or glide like sliding over wet ice: no resistance is experienced. Allow your hands to drift and they will come to rest over some part of the body, usually a short distance from the surface. Sometimes they want to drift away from the body. When this happens I believe that you are being guided to channel Reiki into a person's aura, and I find that after a few moments my hands want to drop back to nearer the body.

With time it becomes easier and easier to detect the subtle and gentle sensations of magnetic pulling and pushing in your hands, and it becomes easier to 'let go' and remove any innate resistance to having your hands moved unconsciously. Imagine that your hands are like those of a puppet on a string, with no resistance to movement. To begin with, your hands may move quite slowly, but with practice they will move with more precision and more purpose.

Using Reiji ho does not mean that you are going to change your way of working so that you spend most of your time hovering your hands over the body: Reiki is basically a hands-on therapy. You simply use Reiji ho as a way of working out where to put your hands. You treat in the intuitively-guided positions and when the feelings in your hands tell you that it is ok to move on to another treatment position, or when you have an impression that you ought to move on to a new position now, you use Reiji ho again to find out where your hands should be placed next. If you have not treated an area sufficiently, your hands will be dragged back there until it has been treated sufficiently!

'Flamboyant' hand movements

Very occasionally you may find that the hand movements that result from allowing the energy to guide you can be a little extreme, or flamboyant, or disconcerting. Perhaps your hands seem to want to drift a ridiculously long way away from the body, or perhaps they want to make long drawn-out movements, or movements that involve vibration of your hands to an extent.

How you deal with this is up to you. You should remember that it is you who is making these movements: you are controlling these movements, or at least your subconscious mind is directing them. If you feel comfortable being a bit more flamboyant with your hand movements then go ahead. If you feel uncomfortable with such movements then simply restrain them. You are in control here.

Using Reiji ho instead of scanning

You may have realised that if you can be intuitively guided to the areas of need, then this lessens the need to use scanning in order to find 'hotspots' (or cool spots, or fizzy spots, or pulsing spots, or breezy spots etc.). If you can work intuitively then your hands will be guided to the right areas to treat, whether or not you can pick up these areas using scanning. Thus if you can work intuitively you don't really need to scan so much, or at all.

In fact you could use Reiji ho as a quick way of scanning the body. See where your hands want to drift: these are the priority areas. Occasionally there will be a big pull to one area of the body, which repeats and repeats: here is an area of great need. In this situation you can say to yourself 'can I be guided to other areas of need please' and see what happens. You should find that your hands will glide to areas of lesser need, which you will end up treating later during the session. It can be a very interesting exercise to try and work out for yourself why your hands have been guided into those positions, and what they are doing there.

But of course we do not need to understand why energy is flowing into a particular area; we do not need to diagnose or interpret. We certainly do not tell the recipient things like "you've got something wrong with your liver": that would be completely wrong. We do not have that knowledge. Energy going into the liver area could be related to the emotion of anger, it could be connected with issues of planning on a mental level, but we would be unwise to tell the recipient that they have 'anger issues' either, because the energy flow may be unrelated to any of these things, and because such information may be unwelcome or unhelpful, or simply incorrect.

In the same way that some people will use scanning quickly at the end of a session to see what has happened to the intensity of energy flow into the 'hotspots', you might also choose to use Reiji ho quickly at the end of a session to see if there are areas of need exerting a big pull on your hands.

Developing your Reiji ho further

I have found through experimentation that it is possible to 'set' your intent, and ask to be guided to areas where there is a need for physical healing, or a need for mental/emotional healing. This is not a method that seems to have come from Japan.

Also, I have found that it is possible to use hands hovering in your imagination only, and these hands will move by themselves to the places where your real hands will subsequently want to go.

By deliberately and consistently making yourself open to intuition, you develop your intuition in general, not just in terms of where your hands should rest when treating someone. So making Reiji ho a regular part of what you do whenever you treat someone, you will enhance your intuitive side in many contexts.

A Reiji ho 'Mudra'

Although there are no specific hand positions associated with this technique, you can use the hand position shown to the left to allow your hand(s) to be

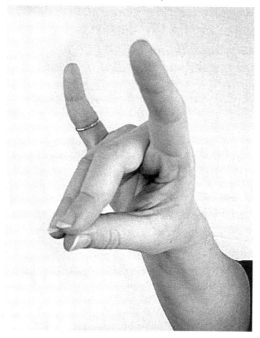

guided more precisely to the area of need. Some people get on very well with this hand position; other people do not like it. Try it for yourself and see what you make of it. Here are the instructions:

1. Put your dominant hand into the position shown.
2. Hover your hands over the recipient with the point downwards.
3. Hold your non-dominant hand palm uppermost, as if to receive energy (optional) or hold both hands in the position shown.
4. Merge with the energy and allow your hands to drift.

Taggart's First Experience of Reiji ho

We worked in pairs, practising on one person on a treatment table. We had our eyes closed. I found that my hands were moved (I did not move them consciously) and my hand kept bumping into the other practitioner's hand, as we were both guided to one specific area!

Secondly, my hand was guided to one specific point and it stopped making wide movements and made very small, precise movements over one small area of the body. The person being worked on had undergone a gall bladder operation in the past and could feel the energy working on the operation scar and on the underlying tissues. I had no knowledge of this condition.

Further practice that same day demonstrated to us that the technique allows you to track the flow of energy along acupuncture meridians, and sometimes our hands were guided repeatedly to track up and down a segment of a meridian. On occasions, the energy moved our hands along a repeated circuit for a while, before moving on to other areas of need. Interestingly, when another practitioner moved to the same part of the body, their hand was guided along the same meridian and the same repeated circuit!

Students' experiences of performing Reiji ho

"Reiji ho: I did seem to feel a pull on my hands when I used Reiji ho on my husband, and ended up in the same areas each time I repeated an area. I didn't feel much pull with my son. After trying for awhile, I did get some pull to a few spots, but never strongly. I had some trouble working with my daughter as well, but then I started feeling tingling in my hands, almost like a directional. By that I mean my fingers would tingle, and if I drifted my hands in that direction (towards where my fingers pointed), it would slowly become a throb in my palm as I got to the "spot". This was different from what I felt with my husband and son, where my hands just drifted on their own.

"...I'm getting along better with Reiji ho. I need to find more people to practice on, but it seems to be coming better now. I even had some luck using it with DH. I drew a rough human outline on paper, and then intended that it represented the person I wanted to send DH to. I used Reiji ho on the sketch, with my hand in a cone shape (to make a smaller point to "aim" with). I was drawn to one area repeatedly. When I checked in with the person, she'd been experiencing pain in the area (I hadn't known about this). "
Karen Small, USA

"During the first few days, I have hardly noticed anything. During a normal treatment, the sensation in my hands are very strong so I was feeling a bit disappointed with the result, but as mentioned one has to be patient and keep practicing regularly. I also think i have tried too hard to feel something and should get used to empty my mind when scanning.

"Here are some of the sensations, I have started to feel by the end of the week : a slight magnetic field on one of the recipient on the chest area as if my hands could not go nearer to the person.

"On the second person, my hand kept being attracted to the knee area - afterwards the person told me that he has constant pain in his knees.

"...Well it has been very helpful to practice an extra 2 weeks. I now completely distance myself by visualizing the photo of Dr Mikao Usui. I do not think about my hands and do not try to feel anything in my hands. Prior to starting Reiji ho, I put my hands in the prayer position and ask the energy to guide my hands.

"1st person: hovering my hands over the chest area, after a few minutes, i am drawn towards the throat. My hands move closer together and slowly near the throat area. Same again when I hold my hands over the head. And during the treatment, the tingling sensation in my hands were the strongest over the throat and she was feeling a lot of heat as well as pins and needles.

"After speaking to her, she was telling me that they wanted to move desperately from the area where they live and make a few changes in their life. However, she did not want to tell her son who is still living at home and has just been treated for cancer of thyroid. She wants to wait until most of the treatment is done but she finds it hard to keep it from him. After several treatments, I have noticed that the sensations are not as strong anymore.

"2nd person: My hands are guided to the stomach area. One hand especially depending on what side of the table I am standing. It seems to glide slowly towards the stomach area. However during the treatment, I do not get a stronger sensation in that area. The heat is at its strongest when treating the head. I know the person and I am aware that he eats a lot of chillies (nearly everyday) and always complains about his stomach/guts. I am still doing full treatments as the signs are improving but are still there.

"3rd person: I have not noticed that my hands were drawn to any particular area, they stay motionless on any of the areas. The person is very healthy in every way, never goes to see a doctor, does a lot of sport, has a healthy diet."
Bruno Cassani, Essex

"I much prefer the Reiji ho method of treatment. It comes far more naturally to me than using any set standard of hand placement. Typically I start off by moving my hands lengthways along the body until I find a change in heat energy. I follow this by going back over the same route, resting my hands on these ' hot spots ' until the energy changes. I repeat this as necessary and then do a final scan.
That's the 'thinking' part, although it's more of a natural routine than thinking. But I have had times when my hands are drawn like a magnet to a particular spot or have gone off in different directions. On one recipient recently, my hands were moving in an almost circular motion in different directions, it felt like a dog trying to sniff out a bone! A couple of times I haven't felt anything at all during a scan."
Deborah Hartley, London

The Power of Intent

Before we leave the subject of treating other people, I want to talk a little about the importance of intent. We have already spoken about intent in the First Degree manual, and you will have realised that when carrying out Hatsurei, for example, while many people will visualise that the energy is flowing down to them, building in their Tanden, flowing out of their bodies to the universe (during Joshin Kokkyu ho), the visualisation is not the important thing. Visualisation is a good way of focusing your intent, but it is the underlying intent that drives the energy, not the visualisation. There are some people who simply cannot visualise, at all, and this is not a problem for them when carrying out Joshin Kokkyu ho because all they need to do is to intend, or to have in mind, that the energy moves in a particular way, and it will.

Where thought goes, energy flows.

Equally, when carrying out the Self-treatment Meditation we can visualise the five special hand positions on our heads, but we can carry out the meditation successfully without visualising, by simply allowing our attention to rest or to dwell on those areas of the head. The energy follows our focus and focuses itself where our attention is directed.

Where thought goes, energy flows.

The significance of this principle can be seen in the following examples:

- If you think nice thoughts about someone, Reiki will follow your focus and that you will be sending Reiki to them, without using symbols or any constructed method.

- You could rest your hands on someone's shoulders and intend that Reiki flows through their body to a particular part of their body; the energy will do that.

- If you intend/imagine that Reiki flows out of your foot chakra then it will do so, and if you intend that this flow of energy stops, then it will stop.

What I am going to do in this section is to describe five exercises or practices that you might choose to use, though none of these practices are actually necessary. The first three exercises are more useful than the last two. You will learn:

1. The 'many hands' technique
2. Beaming Reiki
3. Radiating Reiki
4. Sending Reiki with your eyes
5. Sending Reiki with your breath

The 'Many Hands' technique

This is a way of focusing the energy over a wider area than just the part of the body that is beneath your hands, though of course Reiki does travel from where you send it to where it is needed. This method uses visualisation, but we have already spoken about the importance of your intent and we will show you how you can use this technique even if you can't visualise well.

Let's say that you are treating someone's arthritic knee, or maybe someone had a cartilage operation some time ago: you notice that this area is a hotspot. Both your hands are cupped over the kneecap.

Now imagine that you have an additional set of two arms on each side of your body, making six arms in total (like the Goddess Kali). Feel or become vaguely aware of extra arms coming off your shoulders: upper arms, forearms, with the hands plastered over yours or in slightly different positions near and around your real hands, for example beneath the knee and adjacent to your real hands.

Notice the Reiki energy travelling through your real hands, and now expand this feeling so that you can imagine energy travelling through your accessory hands too. Feel the energy travelling in equal amounts, with as much energy flowing through your imaginary hands as is flowing through your real ones. You may notice that the energy is now flowing more strongly, and often the recipient will be able to feel a difference in intensity too.

This technique becomes easier the more you do it.

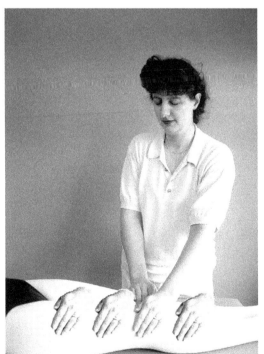

You can even place some extra hands on the ankle and upper leg, or you might imagine a series of hands along the upper and lower leg (coc picture) and this will make the energy you're channelling 'spread out' along the recipient's leg. Often this effect can be noticed by the recipient.

But the visualisation is not the important thing: it is just a useful tool or 'hook' to focus your intent in a particular way. What is important is that you are allowing your attention to rest or to dwell over a wider area of the leg; the energy follows your focus and focuses itself where your attention is directed.

You wouldn't want to use this technique all the time during the course of a treatment, but it can be used selectively, for example when you notice an increased flow of energy in an area: a 'hotspot'.

It is a way of boosting the flow of energy a bit more, increasing the coverage of the energy.

We can use this approach in other areas of the body, too, so you might:

1. Rest your hands by the temples and have imaginary hands hovering in front of the face and cupping round the back of the head.
2. Treat both sides of the body by having real hands resting on the torso, for example, and imaginary hands under the body, mirroring the position of the real hands... cooking both sides of the body at the same time.

'Beaming' Reiki

'Beaming' consists of channelling Reiki at a distance, for example from one side of a room to another. Reiki energy can be seen as coming out of your palm chakras or the ends of your fingers, so you can direct the energy with your palms facing the recipient, or point your fingers at the recipient. You are intending that the energy is transmitted in a particular way, and the energy follows your intent.

What you are doing is a variation of 'projection healing', which is practised by QiGong Masters, who direct chi at specific acupuncture points to treat ailments. In China there is at least one hospital that prescribed QiGong exercises for its patients and has a group of QiGong Masters on hand to treat people by projecting chi. At public demonstrations, QiGong Masters are able to use chi projection to push and pull people off-balance, and you may already have tried this for yourself.

Use beaming to send Reiki to your vegetable patch, your rabbit if you can't catch it, and to calm down irate Rottweilers behind security fencing (make sure they are behind the fence before you attempt this!) Try sitting a friend who has a headache at the end of the room and beam Reiki at them for 15 minutes. See what happens. Beam Reiki surreptitiously under the table to a reluctant recipient (it is always 'for the highest good', remember).

'Radiating' Reiki

If you want to, you can send Reiki out of your whole body. It is not uncommon for people who are being attuned to feel a 'wall of heat' or a 'wall of energy' advancing in front of the Reiki Master, for example. If someone is sitting in front of you, why not intend that Reiki is flooding out of your whole body, not just your eyes, and engulfing the person you are talking to, bathing them in beautiful healing energy. Do this while you are chatting with them.

If you like, try an experiment: have a friend focus on a sad situation or thought/image. 'Connect' with their thoughts and emotions, send them Reiki from your whole body, and see if they can maintain the sad state. Do their state of mind or their emotions change?

Healing through Staring: 'Gyoshi Ho'

For me the important thing about this technique, and the 'breath' technique that follows it, is that they help to demonstrate the importance of intent: if you intend that the energy travels with your breath, it does, and takes on some of the characteristics of breath. If you intend that Reiki passes with your gaze, it does so, and takes on some of the characteristics of staring in terms of being focused, precise and intense. I do not believe that you are actually sending Reiki with your gaze or with your breath when you use these methods: you are simply using a mental 'construct' in order to focus your intent in a particular way.

Both these methods have come to us from the Usui memorial society. It is difficult to say whether Usui actually taught these methods. Certainly he did not teach them to the majority of his students. Perhaps he taught them to the Imperial Officers. This is not clear.

The benefits of conveying energy with the eyes or breath as well as the hand is I suppose that you could 'touch more bases' at one time. You could direct the energy with your hands into two locations, and direct it to a third place using the eyes or the breath. Alternatively, you could intensify the Reiki effect in one place by using two hands and your breath or your eyes. Using the eyes or breath to convey the energy means that you could direct Reiki to places where it would be inappropriate to touch. You could carry out distant healing by sending Reiki with your breath or your eyes onto a photograph, perhaps.

I think that the 'eye' method is more useful in practice than the 'breath' technique.

The key to directing Reiki with the eyes seems to be that you should:

1. Look 'with a loving state of being'
2. Defocus the eyes; look with soft focus
3. Look through the area where we want to send the energy
4. Intend that the energy passes with your gaze

As an exercise, sit with a partner, centre yourself, and look directly through your partner's forehead for a while, with a loving state of being. Imagine that the energy passes with your gaze. What does your partner notice? Now stare through another part of their body; what sensations can the feel now? Now visualise SHK over your partner's face and see if there is any change in the sensations they experience. What happens if you use CKR ?

Healing with the Breath: 'Koki Ho'

The key to directing Reiki using your breath seems to be:

1. Place the tip of your tongue to the roof of your mouth and inhale
2. As you inhale, draw down energy through your crown
3. As you exhale, still with your tongue on the roof of your mouth, intend that energy flows with your breath

As an exercise, sit with any partner, centre yourself, and direct your 'Reiki breath' onto your partner's forehead for a couple of times. You do not need to 'blow a gale' and they do not need to feel air movement on them - the intent is the important thing here. What does your partner notice? Now breathe Reiki onto another part of their body; what sensations can they feel now?

Now you can repeat the exercise, but this time, as you inhale, imagine one of the Reiki symbols (CKR or SHK) on the roof of your mouth, or up in the air above you. Exhale as before onto your partner's face/head. Can your partner feel a difference now, and can they feel a difference between the two symbols? Try breathing Reiki onto other parts of the body. What is the response? Breathe Reiki onto your pets and your plants!

Reiki as a Therapy

Reiki is often presented to the world as a sort of complementary therapy, like Reflexology or Indian Head Massage, and it works wonderfully as a therapy. Some therapists practise Reiki as their main or only therapy, while others offer many different modalities to their clients, including Reiki. If you are thinking about setting yourself up as a Reiki Practitioner, then this section should contain some useful information for you. In the following pages you can find out about these areas:

1. Record Keeping
2. Post-treatment advice sheets
3. Reiki Insurance
4. Reiki Associations
5. Useful Reiki books
6. Useful Reiki web sites
7. Music to use when treating
8. Treatment table suppliers
9. Recommended books about promotion and marketing

In the Appendix to this manual you can also find some information about Reiki and the Law, Health and Safety, and the treating of children.

If you visit our web site you can also find extensive links to a whole range of suppliers.

Record Keeping

It is being suggested in some quarters that Reiki people should be presenting themselves as "healthcare professionals", able to deal with and refer patients to Doctors and liaise with other healthcare providers. For me, such a thing is an attempt to jam a square peg into a round hole. Reiki practitioners are and never will be healthcare professionals. We do nothing other than rest our hands on people and this allow them to move more into a state of energetic balance. We do not diagnose, we do not treat, we do not advise our clients, and our practice has neither scientific basis nor contraindications.

I have seen some Reiki 'client record sheets' that require a more detailed medical history than would be taken by a dental surgeon! This is over-the-top of course. If you wish to see what form of client record sheet, if any, is currently being recommended by the various Reiki Associations then you can find their contact details below.

I suggest that you keep details of any client's name, address and contact telephone number (maybe e-mail address too). On the basis that Reiki might have an effect on the blood sugar levels of some diabetics, and could in theory alter the drug requirement of people with hypertension (high blood pressure), ask them if they have these conditions and advise them to keep an eye on their blood sugar levels after the treatment, or to keep an eye on their blood pressure. To know that a person is epileptic would be useful to you, so that you can ask them what they would like you to do in the highly unlikely event that they had a fit on the treatment table (or maybe you might decide to treat them on a duvet on the floor, for example). There is no evidence that Reiki treatments produce seizures in epileptics, by the way.

Ask them why they have come for a treatment – what is their problem – and record this in the notes. Note the dates when they came for treatments, and anything interesting or unusual that you or they experienced.

I believe that this is sufficient.

What to say at the start of a treatment

When someone new comes for a treatment with you, it is a good idea to explain a few things to them about Reiki, what you are going to do, and what they can expect after the treatment has finished.

You could make these points:

- Reiki is a simple Japanese energy-balancing method that can be used to treat yourself and other people.
- Reiki treatments usually last for about an hour.
- The client lies on a treatment couch, fully clothed, though they should remove their shoes (and maybe belts) for comfort.
- The practitioner rests their hands in a series of non-intrusive hand positions; energy flows through the practitioner's hands into the client.
- The treatment helps to promote deep relaxation and natural healing.
- During the treatment they may feel very relaxed and may even drift in and out of consciousness or fall asleep.
- They may feel heat from the practitioner's hands, or tingling; they may see coloured lights or feel like they are floating, or very heavy.
- They may feel a bit emotional at times, or find that their mind is racing, or that their mind is empty! They may find that some aches and pains come to the surface during the treatment. This perfectly normal.
- The treatment is carried out in silence, and they drift off on the music. Talking will distract the practitioner and the treatment won't be so effective.
- The client should turn off their mobile telephone, as should the practitioner!

- You will let them know that the treatment has come to an end by, for example, resting one hand on their shoulder and turning down the music.

You should demonstrate the hand positions you are going to use so that they know what to expect. If you work intuitively then you can demonstrate the sort of combinations that are likely or possible, and your demonstration will reassure them that hands will not wander into inappropriate positions. At the very least you can show then that you will start with the shoulders, move on to work on the head, and then stand up to work on the torso, finishing with the ankles.

If you are going to spend a little time feeling the energy field or scanning, or using Reiji ho as a scanning method, let them know that to begin with there will be no hands on them for a little while, and that's fine.

What to do at the end of a treatment

Move back from the torso and take a few long, deep breaths. Rub your hands together to 'disconnect'. Then rest your hand gently but firmly on their nearest shoulder. Turn the music down. Say to the client "ok... you can slowly bring yourself back now... and open your eyes".

You might ask them how they feel, what they felt etc. They may ask you what you noticed, and you might comment in general terms about the areas where energy was rushing in bigger amounts, but remember that we do not diagnose and we should not suggest to the client that an area where energy flowed in big amounts represents an area where there is a problem or a disease. You should explain that Reiki works on many levels, so a 'hotspot' over the heart, for example, does not mean a heart problem.

Get a drink of water ready for them, and pass it to them when they sit up on the treatment couch. Help them off the table, or be ready to help them: they may be a bit unsteady.

Explain that they might feel a bit light-headed for a while, or relaxed, or tired, and they may sleep very well this evening. They might experience some emotional ups and downs, or irritability, or some aches and pains coming to the surface; this is normal and nothing to worry about.

Say that Reiki is likely to do something for them, but any effect is not likely to be long-lasting: if they want to get the greatest benefit out of Reiki then they will be looking at, say, 4-6 sessions at weekly intervals. Explain that the effects of Reiki build up cumulatively or gather momentum over time, and 4-6 sessions is usually enough to produce a permanent change, without the need to come along for regular top-up sessions, though they may choose to do this because the treatments feel so nice!

Client advice sheet

It might be helpful if you prepared a brief sheet about Reiki, so the client has something to take away with them after the treatment. Such a sheet could include the following:

- After your treatment you are likely to be feeling relaxed and possibly light-headed. Please ensure that you take the time to recover fully should you have to drive home or operate machinery immediately afterwards.

- It is possible that you may experience some emotional ups and downs, irritability, tiredness or aches and pains after your treatment. This is quite normal and will last only temporarily and should be seen as a positive thing because you are releasing things that you do not need.

- This sort of experience after being treated is common to many complementary therapies.

- Many therapists advise their clients to drink plenty of water, to allow and encourage the flushing out of toxins.

- It is likely that the client will experience some benefit after receiving one Reiki treatment, but to gain the greatest benefit from Reiki they will need a course of treatments, ideally 4-6 treatments at weekly intervals, which allow the beneficial effects to build momentum and become more long-lasting.

Reiki Insurance

You can obtain Reiki practitioner insurance direct from the insurers listed below; you do not need to be a member of any Reiki society or association in order to obtain insurance.

Towergate SMG Professional Risks
SMG House, 31 Clarendon Road, Leeds LS2 9PA
Tel: 0113 294 4000
www.smg-professional-risks.co.uk

Balens
2 Nimrod House, Sandy's Road, Malvern, Worcestershire WR14 1JJ
Tel: 01684 893006 Option 5
Email: info@balen.co.uk
www.balen.co.uk

If you are already a complementary therapist, you may be able to have Reiki 'added' to your existing policy.

Reiki Associations

There is no need to be a member of any Reiki society or association, and most people who practise Reiki won't be a member of any of the following associations. I cannot recommend membership of any of the organisations listed below. In my opinion membership is a waste of money and the societies have some very strange ideas. The two associations listed first below are the biggest ones:

The Reiki Association
Co-ordinator : Sally Smith
2 Spa Terrace, Fenay Bridge, Huddersfield, HD8 0BD.
Tel: 0901 8800 009
E-mail : co-ordinator@reikiassociation.org.uk
www.reikiassociation.org.uk

The UK Reiki Federation
PO Box 1785, Andover, SP11 OWB
Tel: 0870 850 2209
E-mail: enquiry@reikifed.co.uk
www.reikifed.co.uk

The United Kingdom Reiki Alliance
PO Box 114, Stowmarket, Suffolk IP14 4WA
Tel: 01394 388643 (Membership Officer)
E-mail: info@ukreikialliance.co.uk
www.ukreikialliance.co.uk

Reiki Healers and Teachers Society
Tel: 0208 776 0546
E-mail: info@reikihealersandteachers.net
www.reikihealersandteachers.net

Useful Reiki Books

There are many, many books about Reiki on the market today and I have to say that most of them are not worth reading. Most have very little content, what content they do have is inaccurate or misleading or unnecessarily dogmatic; they tell you very little that is useful. Here are a couple of Reiki books that are worth reading, but don't believe everything you read! I have also included a couple of other books that should be of help or of interest to you.

The Reiki Sourcebook
Frans & Bronwen Steine
O Books 2003

Reiki: the True Story: an Exploration of Usui Reiki
Don Beckett
Frog Ltd, 2009

The Japanese Art of Reiki
Frans & Bronwen Steine
O Books 2005

The Miracle of Mindfulness
Thich Nhat Hanh, Rider, London

Mindfulness in Plain English
Bhante Henepola Gunaratana
Wisdom Publications, Boston

Useful Reiki web sites

International Center for Reiki Training	www.reiki.org
Reiki and All Energy-Therapies Web Site	www.aetw.org
The Reiki Threshold	www.threshold.ca/reiki
Reiki Evolution	www.reiki-evolution.co.uk

Music to use when treating

New World Music Limited
Harmony House, Hillside Road East,
Bungay, Suffolk NR35 8RX
Tel: 01986 891600
Fax: 01986 891601
www.newworldmusic.com/uk

Treatment table suppliers

I use New Concept treatment tables and I am very pleased with the quality of them.

Beautelle Supplies Ltd
Beautelle Ltd, Sales Offices & Manufacturing, Unit 1a Railway Terrace,
Nechells Green, Birmingham B7 5NG
Tel : 0121 322 0920
http://www.beautelle.co.uk

Darley Couches
Tel: 01208 873200
www.darleycouches.co.uk

Marshcouch
14 Robinsfield, Hemel Hempstead, Hertfordshire, HP1 1RW, United Kingdom
Tel: 01442 263199
E-mail: nigel@marshcouch.com
www.marshcouch.com

Books about promotion, marketing & running your own business

How to be a Successful Therapist
Celia Johnson
The Book Guild, 2003

Marketing for Complementary Therapists
Steven A. Harrold
Pub: howtobooks 2002

Guerrilla Marketing for the Home-Based Business
Jay Levinson & Seth Godin
Pub: Houghton Mifflin Company, New York

Get Clients Now!
C.J. Hayden
Pub: Amacom 1999

Business Mastery
Cherie M. Sohnen-Moe
Pub: Sohnen-Moe Associates Inc, 1988

Getting Business to Como to You
Paul & Sarah Edwards and Laura Clampitt Douglas
Pub: Tarcher Putnam 1998

Treatment 'techniques'

Western Reiki development has been characterised by endless experimentation and the adding in of principles and approaches from other traditions, and there has been a definite trend whereby originally simple approaches have been made ever more complicated. Experimentation is good, of course: we can discover what is possible and push the boundaries, but the problem comes when we start to rely on more and more 'techniques' which we apply in different situations, and when we start to impose rules about what has to be done and what cannot be done. Then we end up with clutter which takes us further and further from the simplicity of Reiki. Reiki's power comes through its simplicity, and 'complicated' does not mean better or more advanced.

So in this section I have included some ways of working with the Reiki symbols that have been developed in the West. They have very little basis in what Mikao Usui was teaching and I have included them for the sake of completeness. I have also touched on a few techniques that might be helpful to you, and discuss the issues of grounding and protection, issues which seem to be a bit of a preoccupation with some Reiki people.

Here are the main topics to be covered:

1. Western use of the Reiki symbols: CKR and SHK
2. Further novel uses for the Reiki symbols
3. Dealing with low energy levels
4. Focusing energy like a laser beam
5. A Reiki 'detoxification' technique
6. Increasing the flow of energy when you treat
7. Grounding and protection

Western uses of the Reiki symbols

In many Western lineages, CKR is seen as a sort of 'Power' symbol that does not really do anything by itself, but which has to be put on top of other symbols in order to 'empower' them. This principle of putting one symbol on top of another has developed further, so different combinations of symbols are taught, where you draw one symbol, then another, then another etc. Neither of these approaches have anything to do with what Mikao Usui was teaching.

In some lineages the symbols have been tampered with by being reversed, so that some people are taught a CKR that is the wrong way round (CKR should have an anticlockwise spiral) seemingly justified on the basis of a Pagan belief about the properties of spirals, and some people are taught two (or even four) different versions of CKR, one of which is thought to put energy in and the other is thought to take energy out. Again these approaches have nothing to do with Mikao Usui's system, or Dr Hayashi's or Mrs Takata's system either! These approaches can be ignored.

I have included some Western approaches below for information only. Try them if you like, but remember that a simple approach is the best, too much clutter is not helpful, and a reliance on complicated ritual is unnecessary and limiting.

Western use of CKR

Space Clearing

CKR has developed connotations of space clearing, a way of eliminating negative energy from a room. Some people will use CKR routinely to cleanse a treatment room before beginning the treatments each day, or to cleanse a house that you have just bought, or whenever you feel that your house needs an energetic 'spring clean'.

You can do this by using the flat of your hand to draw great big flamboyant versions of the symbol over the walls of a room, the ceiling and floor, and in the centre of the room, saying the symbol's name three times each time you draw it. Imagine that the room is being flooded with vibrant cleansing energy. Some people would choose to draw the symbol in the room's corners rather than the walls; it makes no difference.

Of course you don't need to use CKR in order to space clear: just flood the room with brilliant cleansing white light.

Protection

CKR has also developed connotations of 'protection', so some people will use the symbol to protect themselves, or other people, or property. The symbol might be drawn or visualised over one's car or personal possessions to discourage theft, and might be used to ensure safety during a journey, by the symbol being drawn or visualised over a car or aircraft. People might visualise CKR over themselves as a sort of protective 'shield' in a social situation where they feel they are picking up negative 'vibes' from someone. Some might visualise a protective bubble and see CKR as a way of sealing you in, the bubble allowing positive energy through but deflecting any thing negative, or CKR could be visualised actually over the person or people who are causing the problem, by way of keeping their bad vibes away.

ChoKuRei and Cheap Wine

Buy a cheap bottle of 'plonk' and pour out a couple of glasses as 'controls'. Draw CKR on a piece of paper and stand the wine bottle on the symbol for 10 minutes. Pour out the Reiki'd wine and compare the two. The wine is claimed to now be smoother and sweeter than the controls. Several acquaintances of mine say that they have done this and that Reiki made a real difference to the wine. Try it for yourself!

ChoKuRei and Batteries

Some people see the Reiki energy as being part of the electromagnetic spectrum, though there seems to be no evidence of this as far as I can see. It is suggested that you can charge up batteries by Reiki-ing them. Try Reiki also on dripping taps, tight lids on jars, and jammed doors, using CKR to focus the energy on the physical world, either channelling the energy from that symbol or drawing the symbol over the affected area and letting the energy flow for a while.

ChoKuRei and Food

Take an orange and cut it in half. Put one half to one side on a plate in the kitchen as the control. Put the other half on another plate and give it Reiki, using CKR, every day. Compare the freshness or otherwise of the two. What has Reiki done? The Reiki-ed half is claimed to stay fresh for longer. The Reiki is seen as removing any negative energy from the food. An acquaintance of mine regularly channels Reiki into his food, and claims that salads always to seem more colourful and vibrant afterwards.

Western use of SHK

Positive Affirmations

When you draw SHK over the head some people use it in conjunction with a positive affirmation that you intend is going to be accepted by your client's subconscious. Common affirmations might be 'you are calm, content and serene' or 'you are loved and secure', 'you feel safe', or ' you feel loved and loveable'.

You could slide your hands under the back of the client's head. Use energy from SHK, either by visualising the symbol over the head, or by drawing down SHK energy from above. Focus on their third eye and send the new thought pattern; people would often say the affirmation to themselves three times. Hold this position for about 5 minutes. Alternatively, have one hand at the base of the client's skull, and the other hand resting on their forehead, or rest both hands by the temples.

However, this approach does really go against the notion of stepping aside and allowing the energy to do whatever is right for the recipient with no interference from the practitioner, who is supposed to be neutral in the process, with no expectations and no intention to direct the energy to produce a particular result.

I cannot recommend this practice, and it dubious whether such a practice would be effective in any case.

Other Uses for SeiHeKi

It has been suggested that SeiHeKi can be used in these situations:

1. Spirit rescue (lost spirits who haven't 'travelled into the light')
2. Relationships: use SHK on the two of you as you lay in bed, maybe in conjunction with HSZSN. Always have in mind that you are sending Reiki for the highest good of the people involved: you are not imposing your preferred result on the situation.
3. Use SHK to Reiki your goals, plans, ideas and affirmations: write out the goal, and draw SeiHeKi over the paper. Channel the energy into the paper to empower your goals 'for the highest good'.
4. Use SeiHeKi to help you remember: study some information, and then send SeiHeKi energy into your head, front and back. See what happens.

Further Novel Uses for the Reiki Symbols

Here are some more unusual uses suggested for the Reiki symbols, taken from an Internet Reiki discussion group…

- One of my more elderly students draws the CKR in front of her during her daily swimming session. She swims into it and says it 'lifts' her down the pool and she has been able to increase the number of lengths she completes.

- Just remembered another way I have used it lately. Twice recently when I've arrived at Warren Street Tube station the up escalators have been out of order. Stairs and escalators have not figured greatly in my life since I stopped working in the West End and I viewed the sight of a long, steep staircase with dismay. Not to be outdone, I threw out the CKR with the intention it help me up the stairs and even managed to pass a couple of people on the way.

- I often use CKR's whilst driving and also for giving a boost when unscrewing a top (or in one case opening a stubborn sash window). I figure that if martial artists can use chi to achieve feats of strength, then why not Reiki Practitioners? ;-)

- Someone I know uses it to lift heavier weights in the gym!

- Bouncing golden CKRs along the roofs of the line of cars ahead of you when snarled in a traffic jam.

- Turning right at a busy T-junction, CKR in both directions to create a gap to get through.

- CKR and SHK in advance of a journey to create that parking space.

- I certainly find CKRs work very well with the M25 and I have not been late since I started using them. I also sent Reiki to each day when I was on tour and our coach managed not to break down (unlike the other one, which had a major diesel leak) and each day went very smoothly. I also use it before a performance (I'm a drummer) and it seems to work very well on the old performance nerves!!

- Bearing in mind this discussion, I visualised a little pot or bag in my lap as I was driving, and I sent CKR to lots of little balls or little units of energy in the pot. Then I would pick out one of them and sort of throw it gently at passing cars. Just a gesture of good will. And who knows with what effect?

- I have often used Reiki on the computer. For a while my server was having connection problems, but when I sat there sending CKR to the screen, I almost always was able to connect right away. I used this the other day too when several times in a row the computer crashed as it was loading up. Now it seems all better.

- Have you tried a Reiki bath? It really works!

  - Relax in a deep candlelit bath
  - With hands on either side, and submerged, send Reiki into the water.
  - Lie back and smile

- I use Reiki to help bread and cakes rise - they do not do so well without it!

Treating Low Energy Levels

There are three basic techniques that you can use to treat people who are experiencing low energy levels, and I would include in that people who are suffering from M.E. (myalgic encephalomyelitis). Here are the techniques:

Channelling energy from ChoKuRei

Carry out the majority of treatments using the technique where you channel energy from ChoKuRei. You charge up both hands using ChoKuRei, visualise a large ChoKuRei over the crown of your head, and draw energy from the symbol through the crown of your head, through your shoulders, arms, and out your hands into the person you are treating. The technique is described in detail above.

Reversing the Treatment Direction

The theory here is that when you carry out a conventional treatment, moving from the crown of the head to the feet, you are picking up 'stressed' or 'negative' energy as you go, and this energy is vented from the body, or released, as you get to the ankles/feet. The only problem for people with M.E. is that they have so very little personal energy, even removing or 'grounding' the 'stressed' energy that they have is not going to be particularly beneficial, though Reiki still makes a positive difference to them in many ways. This bit of theory is a bit shaky, but the method works in practice so the theory is not so important.

So to avoid this, work on the feet and move through the hand positions in reverse order, finishing with the head. You can start on the shoulders if you like, to calm everything down and make the person feel really nice and dreamy, but then go to the feet and do your treatment in the reverse direction. I can vouch for the effectiveness of this technique in dealing with M.E., from my personal experience in treating someone with the condition, and other people with low energy levels.

Opening the Foot Chakra

To open the foot chakra, imagine that the chakra looks rather like a flower, with four or eight large petals that can flap open and shut on four/eight sides of the energy centre in the sole of the foot. Contract your Huiyin (see p.84) and use your fingers to brush open each petal a few times in turn, rather as if you were gently brushing aside a small insect from someone's face. You are focusing your intent here, and the precise hand movements are not vital, so you could bunch your thumb and fingertips together and then move them away from each other, imagining that as you open your fingers the chakra opens too.

When you have opened the chakra in one foot, hold your hand over the sole of the foot and channel ChoKuRei for about 10 minutes, visualising the energy travelling up the person's leg further and further. Then open the chakra in the other foot and channel ChoKuRei for another 10 minutes in the same way. Then continue along the length of the body to the head and shoulders.

Focusing Reiki like a Laser Beam

Frank Arjava Petter describes a technique, which it is claimed to be an original Usui technique by a Japanese Reiki stream that is separate from the Usui Reiki Ryoho Gakkai. The 'Gakkai do not seem to have heard of it. This technique does not have a special name. Interestingly, Petter claims that a holy man in India has been seen using just these hand positions in treating someone for toothache, so perhaps the technique is a universal one, not related specifically to Reiki.

The effect of this technique is to convey the energy in a focused form, like a narrow pencil beam torch, or a laser beam, focusing the energy on a very narrow area. It allows greater precision when treating a small area or a specific acupuncture point, a meridian or a foot reflex point, for example, and accelerates the flow of Reiki.

Here are the instructions:

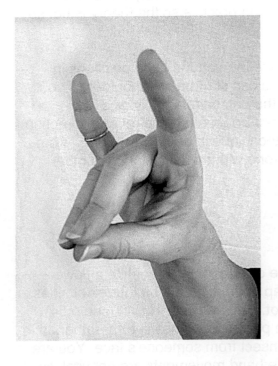

1. With your dominant hand, place the tips of your ring finger and middle finger on the tip of your thumb, with your fingers straight (not curved), leaving your index finger and little finger raised into the air
2. With your non-dominant hand, bunch together the tip of your thumb with the other four fingertips and hold the fingers pointing upwards, by way of receiving energy from above (this part seems to be optional)
3. Use the dominant hand to convey energy in a precise, focused way, concentrating the energy on a small area of need

You may find that shortly after assuming the position described above, you can feel the palm of your dominant hand tingling, as the finger position leads to the energy intensifying and accelerating. Try holding your 'laser beam' fingers 20cm (9") away from the palm of your other hand; draw shapes on your palm using the energy emerging, trace lines of energy up and down your fingers one at a time. Some people can see energy emerging from the three fingertips.

Detoxification technique

The 'Blood Exchange'

Blood Exchange techniques are referred to in Chujiro Hayashi's manual, and seem to be mentioned in Mrs Takata's diary. The techniques are based on the stimulation of the meridian system in such a way that the blood system is said to be replenished, with old red blood cells being eliminated and new ones created to replace them. Interestingly, some research mentioned on William Rand's web site (www.reiki.org) suggests that Reiki treatments can increase haemoglobin levels in patients, but there is no evidence that this technique actually has an effect on blood cells.

The Blood Exchange technique is useful because it seems to help 'bring someone back' at the end of a treatment session, helping someone to become more clear-headed. You don't need to use is, but I have presented it to you out of interest.

Keteuki Kokan (Blood Cleansing Technique)

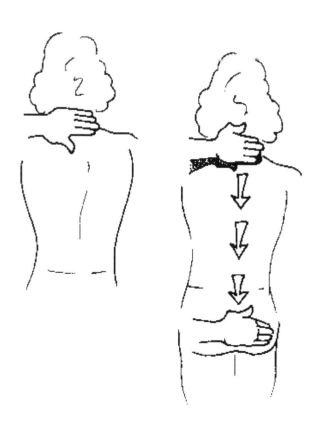

Place your non-dominant hand at the top of the spine and keep It there throughout this procedure. You are going to be making a series of movements along the spine using your other hand, and each time you make the movement, you will start with your hand resting on top of the non-dominant one. Stroke firmly but gently down the spine (hand flat against the back) all the way down to the base of the spine/coccyx, where the hand stops dead. Repeat this 10-15 times. The last time you make the movement, leave the hand

83

at the base of the spine, with the other hand still at the top, and wait until the energy in both hands feels the same – maybe half a minute or so.

Running down the back are the Bladder, Gall Bladder and Governing Vessel meridians, and moving the hand along the back in the way described above would have the effect of stimulating these meridians and dispersing stuck energy, purifying and cleansing. There are special points along the length of one of these meridians that connect with all the major organ systems, and these would be triggered off too. In addition, various branches of the sympathetic nervous system emerge from between the vertebrae on either side of the spine, so they would be affected by your actions as well. The energy touches all bases through this technique.

Increasing the flow of energy when you treat

The Huiyin

Oriental medicine sees a set of 12 pairs of meridians, or energy channels, passing along the length of the body, and an acupuncturist, for example, would take 6 pulses on each wrist to determine which meridian was blocked. As well as these 12 pairs of meridians, they see two extra meridians channelling energy along the front and back of the body in the midline: the functional and governor channels. If it was possible to connect up these meridians then any Reiki coming into you would be channelled out of your hands and would not 'leak out' anywhere else: you would be maximising the benefit of the energy entering your body.

Connecting the Circuit

To connect up this energy circuit you have to contract your Huiyin point (basically your pelvic floor) and press your tongue to the roof of your mouth behind your front teeth; you make an energy circuit that prevents Reiki from leaking out. This means that if you are treating someone when the circuit is made, you will be channelling the maximum amount of Reiki through your hands. With practice (or maybe straight away) you may be able to feel an increase in the sensations from your hands which corresponds with you having made the circuit, though others might feel other effects within their body instead.

Locating the Huiyin point

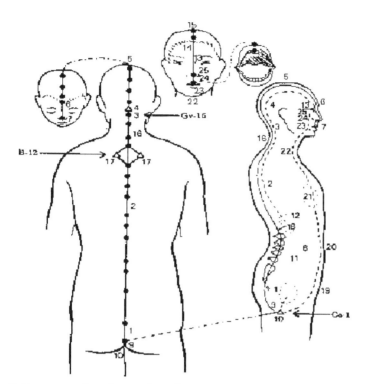

The Huiyin point, or perineum, is located at the pressure point that is felt as a small hollow between the anus and the genitals. The Huiyin point needs to be contracted as if trying to pull the point up gently into the body and held.

Strength of the Contraction

What you should not do is try to attempt some sort of 'Arnold Schwarzenegger' contraction, tensing up all the muscles from the ribcage downwards and stopping you from breathing. This is unnecessary! All that is required is a gentle but definite contraction of a very small part of your anatomy. You can talk and you can breathe quite happily while gently contracting your Huiyin!

Practical use of the Huiyin

Some people recommended that you make the circuit when you are visualising the symbols, whether that be over a person's body, over the walls of the treatment room, or in your imagination. You can certainly make the circuit whenever you want to during a treatment, or indeed throughout all of a treatment, but like the many hands technique it is probably best kept for hotspots. This method can be combined with the many hands technique.

Contracting your Huiyin consistently does take a bit of practice, but it does get easier with repetition.

You don't need to use this technique at all. It has no connection with Usui Reiki, 'Gakkai Reiki, or indeed Hayashi or Takata Reiki. It is one of many non-Reiki methods that have drifted into Reiki in many lineages.

Huiyin and Attunements

Another important point about the Huiyin is that it is contracted throughout the Western-style attunement process in our lineage, so if you're going to be a

Reiki Master and attune people in the Western style, then you will have to be able to contract your Huiyin for long periods. Practice now to prevent hardship later!

Other Energy Techniques use the Huiyin

The use of the Huiyin point is an important part of QiGong exercises, and can be found within Yoga practice also: two different cultures having come to the same conclusion about the energy anatomy of human beings.

Second Degree 'homework'

If you are going to get the greatest benefit out of your Reiki then you are going to have to work at it, by setting aside some time regularly to work with the energy. So below you can find some Second Degree 'homework' for you to carry out. The homework is in four sections:

1. Work on yourself
2. Receive Reiju on Mondays
3. Live the Precepts
4. Work on others

Work on Yourself

The system that Mikao Usui taught was all about working on yourself, and at First Degree level you learned two methods for focusing the energy on yourself:

1. Hatsurei ho
2. Self-treatments – we recommended the self-treatment meditation

Both of these should have been carried out daily.

Now you have learned the symbol meditation, a powerful method to use for self-healing, and this should be substituted for the self treatment meditation at regular intervals. For six months, carry out the symbol meditation more often than the self-treatment meditation, to help to fully get to grips with the energies of earth ki and heavenly ki.

Make these exercises a regular part of what you do, and you will intensify the beneficial effect that Reiki has on you. Your audio CD talks you through Hatsurei ho, the self-treatment meditation and the symbol meditation.

Receive Reiju on Mondays

The system that Mikao Usui established involved receiving empowerments from him again and again. Although it is impractical for you to travel each week to receive an empowerment from your teacher in person, we can echo this regular empowerment practice by you 'tuning in' to distant empowerments that Taggart sends out each week and which you can tune into any time on a Monday.

Perform Hatsurei (or just sit with your hands in the prayer position) and say to yourself "I'm ready to receive my empowerment from Taggart now"… and see what happens! Stay with your hands in the prayer position until you feel that the empowerment is over, or after a few minutes have elapsed.

Live the Precepts

Mikao Usui's precepts were one of the most important parts of his system, and as much spiritual development was said to come through following these as was possible through carrying out energy work. Focus on the precepts each day, remind yourself of them regularly and consider how they apply in your life.

Try to enjoy being in the moment, whatever you might be doing. Try not to dwell on the past and feel bad about things that you cannot change, and try not to dwell too much on the future, either, worrying about things that may never happen! All you have is this moment.

Be compassionate towards yourself, too, which means not beating yourself up for not being perfect, forgiving yourself as you forgive others, being light-hearted and trying not to take yourself too seriously. Be easy-going.

Work on others

The wonderful thing about Reiki is that you can make a positive difference in people's lives, so get out there and plonk your hands on as many people as possible!

If you have your family around you, then practice on them. Rope in your friends and neighbours to be guinea pigs, and see what happens. Tell them that you have learned a Japanese relaxation technique, and that if they have a treatment session with you they will feel so calm, so relaxed, and so stress-free at the end of it. Not many people would say 'No' to that!

You don't necessarily have to carry out hour-long treatments on everybody. Go with what time you have available. Do 15-20 minute treatments on people's heads/shoulders while they are sitting in a straight-backed chair. Do short blasts on a painful knee. Treat your cat, your goldfish and your houseplants. Reiki your salad, and your glass of water, and see what happens!

The important thing is to use the energy regularly.

What you will be doing at Second Degree that is different is to use the energies of CKR and SHK when you treat people, and you will be working intuitively, using Reiji ho. Use Reiji ho whenever you treat someone, and intuitive working will become effortless. Also, you now have a whole range of methods that you can use to send distant healing, a way of experiencing oneness. Experiment to find the approach that feels comfortable to you, and get into the routine of sending distant Reiki to people.

Moving on from Second Degree

You can stay at Second Degree indefinitely if you like, and never move on from this level. If you are thinking of moving on then you have a choice of various courses.

The Reiki Deepening Course

This course is designed for people who want to move on but who do not feel that they want to take the full Master / Teacher course yet. I recommend that you wait for at least three months after completing Second Degree before moving on to this course.

This home study course, taught by Taggart, course focuses on:

1. Enhancing your self-healing and the treatment of others through the use of sacred sounds taught in the original form of Reiki (kotodama)
2. Learning to concentrate energy in your Tanden to enhance your self-healing and self-development
3. Experimenting with both intuition and intent to discover some of the amazing things that are possible.

The Reiki Master / Teacher Course

I recommend that you wait for at least six months after completing Second Degree before moving on to this course, and we would only accept you on one of our RMT courses if:

1. You have been working on yourself regularly, which means regular Hatsurei and self-treatments (either the self-treatment meditation or the symbol meditation)
2. You are comfortable with using CKR and SHK when you treat
3. You are comfortable with carrying out distant healing
4. Your Reiji ho is working well for you.

The interval of six months is also there to give you a chance to get used to working with the greater levels of energy the you channel at this level, to have any 'clear-out' settle down, and to allow you to develop your ability as a channel further.

As well as fully equipping you to pass the gift of Reiki on to other people, using both Western style attunements and original Japanese Reiju empowerments, and providing you with all the support and resources you need to teach others successfully, the benefits to you of Reiki Mastership are in terms of both your self healing and your work on other people:

1. You will learn sacred sounds and meditations that will deepen your self-healing and spiritual development
2. You will learn to further develop your Tanden and how to empower yourself
3. You will learn the use of symbols and sacred sounds to enhance both your treatments and your distant healing
4. You will develop your use of intuition greatly and experiment with intent

Reiki Mastership is not the end of a journey: it is just the beginning of a wonderful and fulfilling journey for you.

Other Reiki-related courses

On the Reiki Evolution web site you will be able to read about further home study and live courses that are available.

In June 2009 we were offering a "Five Element Reiki" course, which is an elegant and powerful healing system that was developed by Taggart and which is open to anyone at Reiki Second Degree.

We also offered various courses that involve using Reiki from s Shamanic perspective, for example the Reiki Drum Technique, Removing Blockages using Reiki, and Cord Cutting using Reiki.

For those who are interested in treating animals, we were offering a two-part Equine Reiki course.

So for those of you who are interested and motivated to learn more, there are various exciting avenues for you to explore and which we can help you with.

Visit the Reiki Evolution web site now and decide how you are going to develop yourself further.

Appendix

I have included below various explanations and articles about things that you may find interesting and useful. Here is a list of the main sections that you can read about:

1. Grounding and protection
2. A brief guide to the chakras
3. Treating children
4. Reiki and the Law
5. Health and Safety Guidelines

Grounding and Protection

'Grounding'

I don't want to make a lot of fuss about the issue of grounding. There are some within the world of Reiki who attribute almost every malady known to man to 'not being grounded', and take many steps at regular intervals to 'ground' themselves and other people. I believe that problems associated with not being grounded are greatly overstated.

When you practise Hatsurei ho you are grounding yourself. When you focus your attention on your Tanden, as you do whenever you practise Hatsurei ho, whenever you treat someone, whenever you moditate on CKR and SHK, and whenever you practise distant healing, you are grounding yourself.

Yes, you can feel a bit spaced out sometimes when you complete a Reiki treatment, and this is more about relaxation and contentment than not being grounded, but doing normal, mundane things grounds one well. Walking outside, doing the washing up: these are grounding practices.

But just for completeness, here is a visualisation that you can use to ground yourself, offered to you with the proviso that you really do not need to do this.

Stand or sit with your feet firmly on the ground. Become aware of the contact between your feet and the floor, and feel a firm, solid contact between yourself and the ground. Now imagine that your feet have turned into roots. These roots push further and further down into the ground, insinuating themselves between rock and clay as they travel further and further into the earth, binding you to the heavy ground beneath your feet. The roots spread out as they go, with more and more branches and rootlets fusing you with the earth. You are heavy and solid.

Go through this visualisation yourself, or if you feel that your Reiki client needs to be grounded, you could talk them through this visualisation at the conclusion of the session, once they are standing or sitting with their feet in contact with the floor.

Protection

In the same way that some people are worrying a great deal about the issue of grounding, there are some people who have been taught to worry a great deal about the issue of 'protection'. A preoccupation with protection is a characteristic of many spiritual healers, and 'protection' issues being raised by Reiki teachers can often be traced to a spiritual healer who subsequently went on to learn and teach Reiki, but who brought with them their spiritual healing 'baggage'.

Reiki and Spiritual Healing are not the same things, and practices that might be thought to be justified in some spiritual healing quarters do not apply to Reiki.

There are various aspects to 'protection', which we can take as meaning 'protection from psychic attack' of some sort, or 'protection from picking things up' from the people we have been treating. Conventional spiritual healers seem to spend a lot of time visualising protective bubbles around themselves, but within Reiki this seems to be a lot less common. I have a friend who runs a healing centre in the Midlands. Her healers fall into two broad groups. There are the spiritual healers, who are quite concerned with protecting themselves from 'astral plane entities' and seem to feel the need to take definite steps to protect themselves as a matter of routine, and there are the Reiki healers who do not feel the need to protect themselves, and who do not experience any problems because of this.

I think that this difference in approach partly comes down to the different traditions and the ways in which the training takes place. I see spiritual healers as alone in the universe, doing what they can through practice and exercises to learn to draw down energy of divine origins. Spiritual healing originated in Victorian Spiritualist Churches, with their table-thumping séances. With Reiki, by way of contrast, you go through a ritual attunement that connects you permanently, and strongly, to a source of beautiful healing energy, and because of this strong and permanent connection, you are protected. Your focus is on the source, not the astral plane.

It is not uncommon for practitioners of hands-on therapies to become quite drained when they treat many clients, or to 'pick up' problems from the people that they have been treating. But Reiki seems to compensate for both of these problems. Reiki boosts and invigorates the practitioner as the treatment is given, so you are not drained or depleted at all by the treatments that you have given. Reiki also seems to protect you from picking up problems from your clients in most cases.

Sometimes Reiki practitioners can 'echo' their clients' problems, by feeling their pain for example during the course of a treatment. However, that is temporary and it is intuition working in a particular way. This is different from the situation where the practitioner walks away at the end of the treatment still experiencing the client's problems.

So it is highly unlikely that you will 'pick up' problems from the people that you treat – the energy flows one way, from you to them – but it is perhaps wise to take simple precautions to guard against this largely theoretical danger. That is why when we finish a treatment we make a ritual disconnection by shaking our hands, clapping or rubbing them together, or blowing through them. You can even say to yourself 'disconnect' if you like. You also know how to use Kenyoku for this purpose, and you might choose to do this after treating someone.

Any form of protection is only as effective as you believe it to be. If you believe that your protection is 100%, then it is. The best protection is serenity, contentment with your life.

Here are some methods that people can use to 'protect' themselves. They are largely unnecessary.

- Imagine that you are surrounded by a transparent energy bubble that protects you from negative energies, but lets positive energies in. The bubble transmutes negative energy into healing energy, and sends healing energy back to the source of the negativity. If you like, you could imagine six five-pointed gold stars around you, as symbols of protection: in front, behind, to the left, to the right, above and below.

- Imagine that you are drawing in your aura around you. Put a deep blue cloak over it and zip the cloak up from under your feet to your chin. Feel that you are completely protected.

- Imagine a flame surrounding you, so that bad thoughts and feelings are burnt up as they come into contact with your radiance.

- Imagine a waterfall flowing from above, washing away any negative energy.

- Imagine the sun shining brightly above you, clearing and nourishing your whole being.

- If you feel that you are getting 'negative vibes' from a person, put up an imaginary mirror facing towards them. The mirror deflects back the bad energy. You can also send the person 'light' to dissolve the negativity.

For the benefit of those of you who wish to delve further into the area of 'psychic protection', here is an article written by a good friend of mine who is a Reiki Master: Chris Burns who started out as a spiritual healer and then moved into Reiki...

Article: "Psychic Protection"

By Christine Burns, Reiki Master

- Have you ever spent time with a person and come away feeling totally drained?
- Have you ever used the expression "You could cut the air with a knife"?
- Have you ever visited a place and not felt completely at ease, regardless of the quality of furnishings or surroundings?

If any of this sounds familiar then the chances are you would benefit from a little bit of psychic protection. But it is not only you that needs protection. What about your family, your home, your car? Everything is open to the influence of the energy surrounding it and that energy can be good, bad or indifferent.

Your words and thoughts create thought-forms of energy that, like absent healing, have no regard for time or distance. If someone thinks about you they create a link. How often has someone come into your mind and shortly afterwards they have telephoned you or you've met them? Pleasant thoughts are excellent but niggling, negative thoughts and words are a form of psychic attack.

When you're out milling around with crowds of other people, perhaps travelling to work in the rush hour, you may find you become very sensitive to the atmosphere. If one person happens to have got out of bed the wrong side, it can be a slippery pole as they collect others in an equally negative mood and together build a black cloud of bad feeling that continues to perpetuate during the course of the day.

So how can you go about creating and maintaining your own, positive space – quietly and discreetly? You just need to change the vibrations.

Auras

Everything has an energy field or aura. Some of you may have seen photographs of auric fields, or be able to see them yourself. Others may be able to sense or feel them. Our energy field vibrates according to our thoughts and physical wellbeing and the vibrations we give out float around in the atmosphere ready to attach themselves to another person or object. If you are in a good mood, then the energy will be pleasant and flowing. If you are feeling decidedly grouchy, or just plain bad tempered, then your energy field is going to be equally as jagged as your nerves.

When energy fields meet, the body registers the experience; a signal is sent to the brain and our body reacts accordingly. Think about that vague, inexplicable feeling you may have had at some time about visiting a certain place or area, one perhaps you have never been to before. There is no particular reason why you shouldn't want to go but for some reason you feel uneasy. You have, in fact, reached out with your aura to the place you are visiting and there is something about that energy field that you are not happy with.

Energy Vampires!

How often have you felt completely drained after being in the company of a particular person? They may have felt a bit down when they met you and have gone off feeling on top of the world and you end up washed out. Energy vampires are expert at latching onto the auric fields of others and draining them because they are unable to 'charge up' their own batteries.

Buildings, furniture, ornaments, jewellery, plants, trees, animals, in fact, just about everything has an energy field. If something has been hand made and the person who made it happened to be having a bad day at the time, then the vibrations of that object will not be at their best.

How do you change the vibrations?

Well, perhaps Prince Charles wasn't so silly talking to his plants. Scientific tests have proven that plants do register positive talk and grow better according to the treatment they receive. As we reach out and sense the energy of a place or person some distance away, so does nature. Hence I have more than a few concerns about genetic engineering in the plant field particularly when it comes to the food chain, but that's another matter.

Having said all that, care should be taken, however, that the hostile energy you believe you are sensing from someone else, isn't coming from you because you have 'typecast' a certain group. People who dress in a certain way (skinheads, for example) are not necessarily 'bad' but because we have heard or read reports of bad behaviour by a few we might tend to feel a bit anxious about them as a group. What we would be sensing in that case would be the fear energy we were projecting rather than what was coming back to us. Your own views on such matters will quickly tell you if it's likely to be a personal hang-up.

Be healthy and not surprisingly you will be protected against a great deal of psychic activity. It's when we're run down that we tend to pick up all sorts of things. Stress, not enough sleep, unhealthy diet, all weaken our aura, as do anger, fear and other negative emotions.

Protection

One very simple but extremely effective form of protection is the auric egg. You simply have to close your eyes, breathe deeply three times to begin to relax and imagine you are inside an egg shaped bubble of light. You must make sure this egg covers the top of your head and goes right under your feet, so that your whole body is surrounded.

As you move around inside the bubble, it seems to have an elastic skin and will stretch in whatever direction you wish. It allows two way traffic for all positive thoughts and feelings, but any negative thoughts sent to you will not pierce the outer skin. You could ask that they are sent back to the perpetrator to give them some discomfort but I prefer to ask that any negative vibrations coming to me are taken away and recycled into positive energy.

Try filling your bubble of light with different colours, or perhaps all the colours of the rainbow. Discover what makes you feel good. If you need a bit of mental stimulation try yellow. A lot of people find blue very peaceful, but don't use it if you feel depressed. Green is calming and balancing. I would not suggest, however, you fill your aura with red otherwise you could find yourself getting very angry and agitated. The best advice when it comes to colours is to remember that a healthy aura contains all the colours.

Should you leave the protective bubble in place at all times?

That, again, is up to you. It is my view that if you only place it there once and then forget about it, it will gradually disappear of its own accord because you will not be giving energy to it. A house that is not lived in gradually crumbles and rots away – there is no loving energy being given to that house. I'm not suggesting you will rot away because you haven't placed your auric egg around you, but there will be times when you will be leaving yourself open to psychic attack. Why not put it on when you get up in the morning and take if off at night when you go to bed, to be washed and cleansed by the Universe whilst you sleep. If you feel that somebody might be sending some negative thought-forms your way, it might also be an idea to place a circle of protective light around your bed at night whilst you sleep.

Do you remember the soap bubbles we used to play with as children? As the sunlight caught them they glistened with all the colours of the rainbow. Well, if you have trouble creating an auric egg around you, think of a giant soap bubble in front of you and simply walk into it. It won't burst and will seal itself once you're inside.

So, you've placed your bubble of light around you but there are times when you still feel anxious. Maybe it's travelling at night when you're alone that worries you. If you're travelling by train, before you start the journey, visualise the carriage being filled with friendly, safe, people who will be with you all the way home, but remember to save yourself a seat!

Create a protector or two to be with you when out walking and call them if you feel uneasy. I suddenly realised one evening when travelling home late that I had a lion and lioness either side of me. Sometimes they become two large black panthers. I don't know why they change, I just trust that is what I need at that time. People certainly keep their distance because they can sense on an energy level that it might not be a good idea to get too close.

Be creative, use your imagination for your protection but never see harm going to anyone as a result of what you do. That's just asking for more of the same to come back to you.

I once found myself under bombardment from unpleasant thoughtforms during the early hours of the morning. My solar plexus felt as if it was being invaded. It was very disturbing and could have been quite frightening. I knew who was sending this energy because I could see them before me. My husband slept peacefully through all this, totally oblivious to what was happening. I immediately placed a gold disc over my solar plexus and surrounded myself with Light. Even so, I knew the thoughtforms were getting into the house.

The next day, I cleaned each room with Light. That night it happened again, although it was much weaker, so I surrounded the whole bed with a circle of Light with an equidistant cross inside it – a very powerful, protective symbol. I had a very peaceful night's sleep.

The following day, however, I 'washed' each room with Light once again and asked the House Angels if there was anything more I needed to do. It was suggested to me that I use a five-pointed star at each window and door. This I did, creating the stars out of Light and asking that they be for the good of all and to harm none and that any negative energies be transmuted by the Light before entering the house. No more problems.

Cars, Houses, Holidays, etc.

If you feel your car is parked in an area where it might be subject to vandalism, surround it with a circle of Light, or the five pointed star, always making sure that the single point is upwards or to the front if used horizontally.

If you're a woman driving alone and you feel vulnerable, apart from using sensible precautions like locking your car doors, invite an Angel of Protection to sit in the car with you, or mentally place a large dog in the passenger seat that will act as your protector. Do remember to thank your protectors and release them once you have completed the journey!

Surround your home with Light. You might want to imagine a beautiful, golden, umbrella of Light over the roof of your house sending down streams of energy.

Going on holiday?

Place a couple of burly security guards at the front and back of the house whilst you're away. Again, remembering to thank and remove them when you get home, otherwise you might end up wondering why no one is visiting you. Whilst talking about holidays, flush out your holiday accommodation with Light when you arrive to disperse any thought-forms left by the previous occupants.

Have you got charisma?

I'm sure we've all met or seen someone who, immediately they walk into a room, seem to have people gravitating towards them. They don't have to be particularly beautiful or handsome but there's something that makes people want to be near them. They are usually oozing with a beautiful energy field that's full of vitality.

So why not use your bubble of Light, gleaming like a diamond, when you're going to a social occasion, particularly if you want to be noticed. Imagine you have a control button inside the bubble where you can turn up the brightness. It can give you tremendous confidence because you will be protected but people will be attracted to you like bees around a honey pot. Conversely, if you want to be quiet and relatively unnoticed, turn down the dimmer switch so the outer edge of the bubble becomes a soft glow.

Clearing energy

The witches broom has become something of a joke in modern times but in Wicca it always had a very serious role and that role was cleaning. The best way to cleanse a room of energy hanging over from a visitor, or your own negative thoughts, is to clean it, particularly the corners - floor and ceiling - where they tend to collect.

Years ago, carpets (if you had one) used to be taken out, put over the line and whacked with anything handy to clean them. Pillows and cushions would be pummelled and floors scrubbed. A great way to disperse energy forms. The pace of living and the modern appliances we have today mean that perhaps we don't go about the job with quite so much gusto but whilst you're vacuuming, washing the kitchen floor, making the beds, see a stream of Light filling everything.

Common sense

Last but not least, please use common sense – the greatest energy of all to my mind – when deciding you need to use protection. Energy follows thought. Think about that for a moment. Whatever you dwell on stands a pretty good chance of being brought into being, particularly if you put a lot of emotion into that thought. So please don't go around imagining that every dark corner holds a danger. You, obviously, are not going to place yourself in a difficult situation just to see if the energy works. Use the energy wisely, as you would do any other safety measure but with positive thinking and an abundance of Light around you, the chances are you're only going to attract good things anyway.

May all that happens to you be for your Highest Possible Good.

Christine Burns

Chakras

The chakras are a way of viewing the human energy system. In Oriental Medicine they see a system of pairs of energy channels or meridians, with various points along the length of them that can be stimulated using needles, or heat, or finger pressure. In India they see a system of energy centres along the length of the body from the crown of the head to the base of the spine which can be developed and balanced using such things as exercise (yoga) and meditation. The word chakra means 'wheel' in Sanskrit and the chakras are seen a spinning vortices of energy. People usually think in terms of seven main chakras, as follows:

CROWN - THIRD EYE - THROAT - HEART - SOLAR PLEXUS - NAVEL - ROOT

Each chakra is said to have an associated colour and organ system. In fact there are a whole range of correspondences related to each chakra. There are endless books written about the chakras and the things they correspond to. Read some books about them If you are interested, and read about Traditional Chinese Medicine too.

Usui Sensei would not have thought in terms of chakras. This is a New Age preoccupation and because Reiki travelled with the New Age movement for many years, and still does to an extent, chakras can turn up on Reiki courses, with various techniques having been developed to focus Reiki on the chakras.

For example, some people are taught quite complicated procedures for using Reiki to balance the chakras. Such things are unnecessary. Reiki will help to balance people's chakras even if the practitioner has never heard of Chakras: they are a basic part of our energy anatomy, so how could Reiki fail to bring balance to them?

Chakra correspondences

A chakra may be seen as 'open', or spinning in a balanced fashion. It could be seen as 'closed' or spinning sluggishly. It could be seen as spinning too fast, though this seems to be less common in my experience.

What I am going to do first of all is to describe the mental and emotional characteristics that accompany 'closed' or sluggishly spinning chakras. When you are treating a person and your hand is over one of the chakra positions, and when you feel a lot of energy flowing into that area, this suggests that – assuming the energy is actually working on the chakra - it may be 'closed' or spinning sluggishly and needs Reiki energy to become open. The energy can be seen as dealing with the, or some of the, mental/emotional associations of that chakra.

Try and perceive whether the energy is working on someone's chakra rather than any physical part of him or her. What impression do you get?

As with all things, do not take these associations as dogma to be read out to the patient at the end of the treatment session. Be careful about what you say to people until you are confident in your ability to perceive. Think carefully about the chakra associations, about what you know about the person you are treating, think carefully about the energy sensations you are experiencing in the different treatment positions, and whether some associations may seem more appropriate than others for this person. You might be better advised to say nothing, to watch and to learn.

When the Chakras are closed

Root chakra closed
Emotionally needy, low self-esteem, self-destructive behaviour, fearful

Sacral chakra closed
Oversensitive, hard on him/herself, feels guilty for no reason, frigid or impotent

Solar Plexus chakra closed
Overly concerned with what others think, fearful of being alone, insecure, needs constant reassurance

Heart chakra closed
Fears rejection, loves too much, feels unworthy to receive love, self-pitying

Throat chakra closed
Holds back from self-expression, unreliable, holds inconsistent views

Third eye chakra closed
Undisciplined, fears success, tendency towards schizophrenia, sets sights too low

Crown chakra closed
Constantly exhausted, can't make decisions, no sense of 'belonging'

The above descriptions are the most useful ones, because they tie in emotional characteristics to areas of increased energy flow in the various chakra positions that you could potentially experience in your hands. Moving on from this, the next sheet describes the associations that could be relevant when the chakras are open and balanced. Do these associations describe a person who has no hotspots and is not drawing huge amounts of Reiki energy?…

When the chakras are open and balanced

Root chakra open
Demonstrates self-mastery, high physical energy, grounded, healthy

Sacral chakra open
Trusting, expressive, attuned to his/her own feelings, creative

Solar Plexus chakra open
Respects self and others, has personal power, spontaneous, uninhibited

Heart chakra open
Compassionate, loves unconditionally, nurturing, desires spiritual experience in lovemaking

Throat chakra open
Good communicator, contented, finds it easy to meditate, artistically inspired

Third eye chakra open
Charismatic, highly intuitive, not attached to material things, may experience unusual phenomena

Crown chakra open
Magnetic personality, achieves 'miracles' in life, transcendent, at peace with self.

Finally, the next sheet describes the associations for people whose chakras are spinning too fast. This seems to happen a lot less frequently than slow spinning or closed chakras, in my experience. It is not really possible for a Reiki practitioner to become aware of fast-spinning chakras other than through dowsing using a pendulum, or perhaps by making a connection between a person's mental/emotional state and the associated chakra. But remember that Reiki is not a diagnostic system. When we treat someone we are there to simply allow energy to flow into the recipient. We are not there to advise people.

When the Chakras are Spinning too fast

Root chakra spinning too fast
Bullying, overly materialistic, self-centred, engages in physical foolhardiness

Sacral chakra spinning too fast
Emotionally unbalanced, a fantasist, manipulative, sexually addictive

Solar Plexus chakra spinning too fast
Angry, controlling, workaholic, judgmental and superior

Heart chakra spinning too fast
Possessive, loves conditionally, withholds emotionally 'to punish', overly dramatic

Throat chakra spinning too fast
Over-talkative, dogmatic, self-righteous, arrogant

Third eye chakra spinning too fast
Highly logical, dogmatic, authoritarian, arrogant

Crown chakra spinning too fast
Psychotic or manic depressive, confused sexual expression, frustrated, sense of unrealised power

Treating children

When treating children, there are a couple of things that you need to keep in mind.

Firstly, if giving Reiki to a child it would be a good idea to obtain the signed permission of the child's parent or guardian, and this permission should be kept with the client's notes. A suitable form of words is below:

I hereby agree to my child.. aged................receiving Reiki treatments from the person named below.

Reiki practitioner's name...

Parent/guardian's signature...

Date.......................

Secondly, since it is against the law for a parent or guardian not to seek medical treatment for a child under the age of 16 years, if a child needs medical attention and the parent or guardian refuses to obtain it, then the practitioner should obtain a signed statement from the parent or guardian, to the following effect. The statement should be signed and dated by both the parent or guardian and a witness and kept in the client's records.

I have been advised by..that according to the Law, I must consult a doctor concerning the health of my child.

Name of child...

Signed..(parent or guardian)

Signed..(witness)

Date......................................

In such circumstances it might be better to refuse to treat the child.

The Reiki Practitioner and the Law

Provided by Susie Jennings, Reiki Master / Teacher

In England the law is divided into two main categories: Criminal Law and Civil Law. Criminal law is contained in Acts of Parliament and if a person contravenes Criminal Law he is prosecuted by the State. If found guilty, the offender may be fined or imprisoned. Civil Law concerns the rights of citizens in their relationship to one another and action is initiated by the injured party. If the claim succeeds, the offender is ordered to pay damages for redress of injury.

The Prohibited Appellation Act - This Act makes it a criminal offence for anyone who does not hold the relevant qualification to use any of the following titles: chemist, chiropodist, dental practitioner, dental surgeon, dentist, dietician, doctor, druggist, general practitioner, medical laboratory technician, midwife, nurse, occupational therapist, optician, orthoptist, pharmacist, physiotherapist, radiographer, remedial gymnast, surgeon, veterinary practitioner, veterinary surgeon.

The Prohibited Functions Act -This Act prohibits unqualified persons performing certain specified functions in the field of medicine: dentistry, midwifery, veterinary surgery and for the treatment of venereal disease. The only exception would be helping a woman in childbirth only in cases of sudden or urgent necessity.

Fraudulent Mediumship - The law stipulates that anyone who purports to act as a spiritualistic medium or to exercise any power of telepathy, clairvoyance or other similar powers with intent to deceive is guilty of an offence.

AIDS - It is for the individual practitioner to decide whether to give treatment to an AIDS patient.

Wilful and Reckless Exaggeration - of ones abilities and skills is held in law to constitute fraud. It is therefore vital that practitioners should exercise great restraint in describing their own abilities and also the benefits of reiki.

Advertising - The law makes it an offence to refer in an advertisement to any article or service in terms which are calculated to lead to the use of that article or service for treating human beings for any of the following diseases: Bright's Disease, Glaucoma, Cataract, Locomotor Ataxy, Diabetes, Paralysis, Epilepsy or fits; Tuberculosis. There is, however, no prohibition on treating a client for the foregoing diseases, the offence is in advertising treatment.

It is an offence to publish any advertisement which offers to treat, to prescribe a remedy for or give advice on the treatment of cancer, or refers to any article or service in terms calculated to lead to its use in the treatment of cancer. It is not an offence to treat a client with cancer, it is an offence to advertise treatment or a cure for the condition.

At all times advertising should comply with standards laid down by the British Code of Advertising Practice and meet the requirements of the Advertising Standards Authority.

The Treatment of Children - It is an offence for the parent or guardian of a child under 16 to fail to provide adequate medical aid for the child. The law does not prohibit a practitioner from treating children. However, to avoid being charged with the statutory offence known as ' aiding and abetting ', the reiki practitioner should explain to the parent or guardian the nature of the obligation imposed by law and request them to sign a disclaimer (see accompanying disclaimer).

Professional Negligence - The only Civil Law to which practitioners are subject is an action for damages for professional negligence. The meaning of negligence in English law is, very broadly, that in any contract with other citizens a person must have regard for their interests and that, if through some act of commission or omission committed without sufficient regard for another person's interest, that other person sustains injury, he is liable to pay damages as monetary redress for the injury inflicted.

The relationship of practitioner and client automatically imposes on the practitioner a duty to observe a certain standard of care and skill in the treatment or advice he gives. Failure to attain to that standard exposes the practitioner to the risk of an action for damages.

A 'professional' person is by definition one who professes to have certain specialist knowledge or skill not possessed by the layman and, in general, a practitioner of any profession is bound to possess and exercise the knowledge, care and skill of an ordinary competent practitioner of that profession. Professional negligence may take one of two forms; either lack of requisite knowledge and skill to provide the treatment offered, or else, while possessing the necessary knowledge and skill, failure to apply it properly.

It will therefore be seen that the knowledge and skill which reiki practitioners profess to have, is of crucial importance in the context of professional negligence. It is essential that practitioners do not claim to possess knowledge, or purport to exercise skills, they do not possess.

It should be an essential part of training to ensure that every practitioner is aware when a case is beyond the scope of his/her particular skill and when to call in a more skilful person, to refer the client to a medical practitioner, another therapist or to ensure that the client no longer relies exclusively on his skill alone.

False and Misleading Statements - The law on this subject was greatly expanded by the Misrepresentations Act 1967 and the Trades Description Act 1968.

Under the 1967 Misrepresentations Act - If a client engages the services of a practitioner, and pays fees for the treatment which proves unsuccessful, having been induced to engage the practitioner's services by a misrepresentation made by the practitioner about the efficacy of the treatment, the client could recover those fees (and any other expenses incurred as the result of the lack of success of the treatment) as damages for breach of contract.

Under the 1968 Trades Description Act - Any statement about the properties of goods or the nature of services offered which is false, misleading or inaccurate can give rise to prosecution.

As reiki practitioners do not sell or supply goods, the relevance of this Act is in the provisions concerning false statements as to services. This includes false statements about the effect of the treatment.

It would therefore be unwise for a practitioner to claim he could cure or diagnose or make any statement about qualifications and experience unless it is true and can be proved to be true.

Insurance - Any individual wishing to practice as an alternative or complementary therapist should ensure that he/she is adequately insured to practice. Such insurance should cover public liability and professional indemnity against malpractice. Failure to do so could result in disciplinary procedures from the membership body to which the reiki practitioner belongs and also payment of any legal costs should the case be successful.

Premises - A practitioner carrying out a profession from any premises should ensure that his/her treatment room and any facilities to which members of the public have access are fully covered by any public liability insurance. Practitioners working from home should give special attention to the terms of their lease or other title deeds and any local government regulations limiting such practice or requiring the premises to be licenced. The Trading Standards and Environmental Health Departments of local authorities have a variety of information leaflets on legislation.

Health and Safety at Work Act 1974 - The Act requires employers to provide systems of work that are, so far as is reasonably practicable, safe and without risk to health. All equipment must be safe and checked regularly, the environment must be kept free of toxic fumes, fire fighting equipment should be accessible and in good working order, first aid supplies available, exits unobstructed and access possible for disabled people. Employees have responsibilities to take reasonable care of themselves, and any other people affected by their work, not to misuse any equipment and to co-operate with their employers in the discharge of their legal obligations.

Notifiable Diseases - It is a statutory requirement that certain infectious diseases are notified to the Medical Officer of Health of the district in which the client resides or in which he is living when the disease is diagnosed. The person responsible for notifying the MOH is the GP in charge of the case. If, therefore, a practitioner were to discover a notifiable disease that was clinically identifiable as such, he should insist that a doctor be called in. Each local authority decides which diseases shall be notifiable in its area. There may therefore be local variations, but it is assumed that the following diseases are notifiable everywhere.

Acute encephalitis	Leprosy	Scarlet Fever
Acute meningitis	Leptospirosis	Tetanus
Acute poliomyelitis	Malaria	Tuberculosis
Anthrax	Measles	Typhoid Fever
Cholera	Opthalmia	Typhus
Diphtheria	neopatorum	Whooping Cough
Dysentery	Paratyphoid Cough	Yellow Fever
Food Poisoning	Plague	
Infective Jaundice	Relapsing Fever	

Legal Advice - Any practitioners who find themselves faced with the possibility of legal proceedings whether criminal or civil and however remote, should contact their professional organisation for advice.

Further Legal information

This information is as published by the UK Reiki Federation.

1. A parent or guardian who wilfully fails to provide adequate medical aid for a child under the age of 16 may be committing a criminal offence. Reiki is not defined as a medical aid by law so anyone who treats a child whose parents refuse medical aid could be seen to be aiding and abetting that offence. When treating a child it is advisable to secure the signature of the parent or guardian to the following statement: "I have been warned by (Reiki practitioner's name) that according to Law I must consult a doctor concerning the health of my child (child's name)." This statement should be signed and dated by both parent or guardian and a witness and kept within the client records.

2. It is illegal to practice dentistry if unqualified. Hovering your hands over someone's face doesn't constitute the practice of Dentistry anyway! Taggart's Note: Reiki will only give temporary pain relief; the underlying disease process will continue.

3. It is advisable to not knowingly give Reiki to people who are suffering from syphilis, gonorrhoea and soft chancre. Under the Venereal Diseases Act 1917 it is illegal to treat any of these conditions for reward, whether direct or indirect. Any service must be provided entirely for free.

4. It is an offence to offer treatment or prescribe a remedy or advice for cancer.

5. Any advertising should comply with the British Code of Advertising Practice and meet the requirements of the Advertising Standards Agency. Adverts should be dignified and should not claim a cure or mention any disease.

6. Except in cases of urgency or sudden necessity it is illegal for anyone other than a certified midwife to attend a woman in childbirth without medical supervision or for anyone other than a registered nurse to attend for reward as a nurse on a woman in childbirth or during a period of 10 days thereafter.

7. Reiki practitioners should not prescribe or sell remedies, herbs, supplements, oils etc. unless they have undergone appropriate training and have qualifications which entitle them to do so.

8. Before treating animals it is advisable to seek assurance from the owner that a vet has examined the animal. The Veterinary Surgery Act 1996 prohibits anyone other than a qualified veterinary surgeon from treating animals, including diagnosis of ailments and giving of advice on such diagnosis. However the healing of animals by contact healing,

by the laying on of hands and distant healing, is legal. However the Protection of Animals Act 1911 requires that if an animal clearly needs treatment from a veterinary surgeon the owner must obtain this. To give emergency first aid to animals for the purpose of saving life or relieving pain is permissible under the Veterinary Surgeons Act 1996 Schedule 3.

9. It is required that cases of certain infectious diseases are notified to the Medical Officer of Health in the district in which the client is resident. The notification must be made by a GP, so if a Reiki practitioner suspects that the client is suffering from a notifiable disease they should insist that the client should see a doctor.

10. Notifiable diseases under the Public Health (Control of Diseases) Act 1984 are as follows: Cholera, Plague, Relapsing Fever, Smallpox, Typhus, Food Poisoning.

11. Under the Public Health (Infectious Diseases) Regulations 1988 the diseases are as follows: Acute Encephalitis, Acute Poliomyelitis, Anthrax, Diphtheria, Dysentery (Amoebic or Bacillary), Leprosy, Leptospirosis, Malaria, Measles, Meningitis, Meningococcal Septicaemia (without Meningitis), Mumps, Opthalmia Neonatorium, Paratyphoid Fever, Rabies, Rubella, Scarlet Fever, Tetanus, Tuberculosis, Typhoid Fever, Viral Hemorrhagic Fever, Viral Hepatitis, Whooping Cough, Yellow Fever.

12. Reiki practitioners must investigate and co-operate with local by-laws and all relevant Health and Safety legislation.

Reiki in Hospitals

All Reiki practitioners visiting Hospitals should comply with the guidelines laid down by the British Complementary Medicine Association (BCMA). The hospital is responsible for the patient. Reiki practitioners may only treat patients in hospitals with permission from the patient, the hospital authority including the ward charge nurse. Reiki practitioners should not wear clothing which gives the impression that they are a staff member of the hospital. They may have some sort of identification such as a lapel badge. Where permission is given to provide treatment on the ward, this must be carried out without fuss or interruption to other patients and staff. If other patients request treatment, the permission of the ward charge nurse, nursing officer (and if relevant, the patient's doctor) must first be obtained. Reiki practitioners should never undermine the patient's faith in hospital treatment or regime. Where credentials are requested, Reiki practitioners must provide their associated current membership card or other proof of membership and permission to visit.

Health and Safety Guidelines

Provided by Sue Jones, Reiki Master / Teacher

This is a quick guideline to the Health and Safety requirements of running your own Reiki business. It must be noted that this is for a self-employed person who does not have any employees.

Britain's Health and Safety Commission (HSC) and the Health and Safety Executive (HSE) are responsible for the regulation of almost all the risks to health and safety arising from work activity in Britain. The HSE website – www.hse.gov.uk – is a wealth of information, or if you have any questions you can call them direct on their Info Line 0845 345 0055 (they are very helpful), or to order a free copy of any booklets mentioned in this guide, call 01787 881165.

British Health and Safety law requires that you carry out certain duties to ensure that you, your client and members of the public are working and enjoying a Healthy and Safe environment. To this end, I have compiled the list below as guidance to these duties.

Risk Assessments

A Risk Assessment is nothing more than a careful examination of what, in your work, could cause harm to people, so that you can weigh up whether you have taken enough precautions or should do more to prevent harm.

In Reiki, this could be someone falling from the massage couch that you use, to someone falling down the stairs if you use an upstairs room in your home.

Risk Assessments are very easy to compile; first you need to list the hazards, then the people who might be at risk from the hazards, and then list controls you have to ensure that the risks are minimized.

So, someone falling off the couch is the hazard, the client would be the person at risk from the hazard, and the controls you have to ensure the risks are minimized are that you assist people on and off the couch and let them take their own time to sit up on the couch after a Reiki session.

HSE Booklet 'Five Steps to Risk Assessment' contains further information.

Manual Handling

Manual Handling covers a wide variety of tasks including lifting, lowering, pushing, pulling and carrying. It is important that you Risk Assess any tasks that you do that include any of the above. If you carry your massage couch about with you to give treatments, it is advisable that you complete a Risk

Assessment, to show that you have considered the risk involved in carrying the couch and have taken reasonable steps to ensure your safety.

HSE Booklet 'Getting to Grips with Manual Handling' contains further information.

Riddor

Riddor stands for the Reporting of Injuries, Diseases and Dangerous Occurrences Regulations 1995. If you are an employer, self-employed or in control of work premises, you will have duties under Riddor.

Riddor requires you to report some work-related accidents, diseases and dangerous occurrences. It applies to all work activities. If you have a work-related accident and are off work for more than three days, if a member of the public is killed or taken to hospital, if there is a dangerous occurrence or your doctor informs you that you have a work-related disease or condition, you will need to report it to the HSE within 10 days.
It must be noted that for most businesses, a reportable accident, dangerous occurrence or case of disease is a comparatively rare event, but it is important that you are aware of your duties in this instance.

HSE Booklet 'RIDDOR' contains further information.

Slips & Trips

Slips and trips account for 33% of all reported major injuries, therefore it is always important that you take into account the floor surfaces that you are working on. If you use your own premises for treatment, it is always a good idea to do a Risk Assessment to highlight any potential dangers and allow you to minimise them.

HSE Booklet 'Slips, Trips & Falls' contains further information.

VDUs

If you use a computer to do your work, you will need to ensure that you have a comfortable workstation and that you take breaks between working on your computer.

HSE Booklet 'Working with VDUs' contains further information.

Use of Electrical Equipment

If you use Electrical Equipment during your sessions, you have a responsibility to ensure that the equipment is well maintained. This can be done by a regular visual inspection, to look for visible signs of damage or faults, and where necessary have the equipment tested by a professional.

HSE Booklet 'Electrical Safety and You' contains further information.

The Provision and Use of Work Equipment (PUWER)

Like the use of Electrical Equipment, this regulation is designed to ensure that you use suitable equipment for the job you do, and that it is well maintained. Again, a regular visual inspection to look for visible signs of damage or faults will be required.

HSE Booklet 'Simple Guide to the Provision and Use of Work Equipment' contains further information

Insurance

While the HSE only enforce the requirement of Insurance if you employ people, they do strongly advise that you take out insurance to cover yourself for Professional Indemnity and, if you use your own premises, you will need to take out Public Liability Insurance.

Health and Safety Policy Statements

On a side note, I was informed by the HSE that while it is not a requirement for a self-employed person with no employees to have a Health and Safety Policy Statement, it is considered good practice to have one. A copy of a policy statement can be found, along with a Risk Assessment example, in the HSE booklet 'An Introduction to Health and Safety'.

It must be remembered that the above is a guide only, and that Health and Safety Regulations and Requirements are an ongoing venture. It is your responsibility to ensure that you have kept up to date with any changes in the laws concerning Health and Safety.

Another booklet that you might find helpful is 'Health and Safety Regulation... A Short Guide'.